INFERTILITY SUCCESS

MORE Stories of Help and Hope for Your Journey

By

Erica Hoke

Harmony Bacon, Erin Banks, Raylene De Villiers,
Cara Drescher, Dr. Patrick & Christy Flynn,
Angela Kelleher. Ilonka Markram, Courtney Mae
Ripoll-McBride, Susan Tozer, Wendy Vermaak
With Forward by Dr. Stephan Volschenk

Copyright © 2023 Erica Hoke
1st Edition
Copyright © Sarasota, Florida

ISBN
Print 978-1-7375522-2-2
e-Book 978-1-7375522-2-2

All Rights Reserved
For Permissions email erica@ericahoke.com
No part of this book may be reproduced in any form or by any electronic or mechanical means, including information storage and retrieval systems, without written permission from the author, except for the use of brief quotations in a book review. All information shared in these chapters are the authors personal experiences and are not meant to treat, diagnose, or cure any illness or disease. Please consult your physician with any questions about procedures, tests or supplements mentioned here.

Editing by Melissa Denelsbeck
Cover Design: Meraki

CONTENTS

Foreword v

A $10 Antibiotic: An Unexpected Cure to My Infertility 1
Erin Banks

It's a Journey, Hold On (to Hope) 17
Wendy Vermaak

I Disagree 28
Dr. Patrick and Christy Flynn

What Happens to the Heart? 39
Angela Kelleher

By the Moon and the Stars 51
Raylene de Villiers

Secondary Infertility: Our Journey of Hope 63
Ilonka Markram

Preparing Elliana's Womb 76
Harmony Bacon

Vicious Cycles to Vibrant Rainbows: My Story of Navigating
Infertility, IVF, Triplets, and Motherhood with Twins 89
Cara B. Drescher

A Veteran's Journey to Conception: Navigating Infertility
Treatment and Resources with the VA 107
Courtney Mae Ripoll-McBride

BONUS CHAPTERS FROM
Infertility Success, Stories of Help and Hope for Your Journey 121

To Hell and Back: A Journey to Motherhood 122
Susan Tozer

Seven Diagnoses and Seven Years to Four Sons.............133
Erica Hoke

Acknowledgment 147

FOREWORD

People keep saying, "Relax, go on holiday, stress less," or they say, "When are you going to start a family?" How many times have people who are struggling to conceive had to listen to this and other similar platitudes? They are innocent comments made by friends and families who have no harmful intent, but these comments are more often than not emotionally devastating to the person/people on their own respective fertility journey.

If you are reading this foreword, you are more than likely one of the people on the receiving end of those comments, or at least you know someone who is going through this very difficult journey. If so, keep on reading and do not stop until the last word of the last paragraph. A book of this caliber has been long overdue and reading it made me realize how important this book will be for many people. Nothing speaks more to the heart, makes it more real, and gives more insight into the painful journeys of each of the individuals who contributed to this book. Sharing their very unique journeys in the ways they do is very brave and deserves much respect and admiration. No matter what the ultimate outcome was, happy or sad, the pain never goes away.

You may be asking how I can say all the above with so much conviction. As a dedicated reproductive medicine specialist for the past 19 years, I have attended to thousands of patients suffering with infertility, and I have traveled these journeys with each and every one of them. Therefore, I really do understand how painful these individually unique fertility journeys can be. I keep on referring to "journeys" because they are journeys. They are journeys filled with many invasive medical procedures. They are long journeys that most of the time seem to be never ending. They are journeys that are emotionally and completely destructive. They are journeys that test one's ability to survive to the utmost.

Contrary to popular belief, these journeys do not consist of just very invasive medical procedures but also lots of emotional trauma and insecurity. The latter is a very important part of fertility treatment and, in most cases, turns out to be the most difficult part of the journey. It is, therefore, very important to realize that not only does one have to be physically fit and able but also emotionally and psychologically stable and strong.

I always say to my patients, "If the vessel is not whole and complete in every aspect, then it cannot leave the harbor to travel the ocean of infertility management successfully." Therefore, do not just focus on the medical procedures in the doctor's office or fertility clinic, for these procedures alone will not bring success. Focus on everything, both internally and externally. Fix what needs fixing physically and emotionally. Gain strength in failure and never ever give up. For beyond the horizon lies ultimate success, joy, and happiness.

Enjoy this wonderful and insightful book. I know that I definitely did!

Dr. Stephan Volschenk
MBChB (Pret) Cum Laude MMed O&G (Pret) Cum Laude
F.C.O.G. (S.A.) with Reproductive Medicine

Dr. Volschenk has dedicated his career to managing patients with infertility. In 1986, he earned his medical degree Cum Laude from the University of Pretoria. Following this, he completed both orthopaedic and general surgery rotations at Tygerberg and Grootte Schuur Hospitals before going on to practice as a general practitioner in Namibia until 1997.

In 2001, Dr. Volschenk returned to Pretoria to complete his specialist degree in Obstetrics and Gynaecology- Cum Laude- and then honed his skills through additional training in laparoscopic surgery at Leuven in Belgium. In 2002, he joined the Fertility Unit at the University of Pretoria but continued to expand his knowledge in the field of infertility by traveling to Kiel, Germany and Copenhagen, Denmark. Finally, in September 2003 he joined Vitalab Centre for Assisted Conception where he has practiced as an infertility specialist ever since.

"Managing patients suffering from infertility has always been a calling for me and will forever be going forward," said Dr. Volschenk about his passion for helping those struggling with fertility issues.

A $10 ANTIBIOTIC: AN UNEXPECTED CURE TO MY INFERTILITY

Erin Banks

I'm here to share with you the most wicked journey I've ever experienced. Infertility. Taking this journey does not define you. It's not your whole story; it's a chapter in your story.

I was fortunate to conceive my first baby naturally; this is my story with secondary infertility.

My husband and I decided we were ready to start trying for our first baby in July so I had my IUD removed. I had been on birth control pills since I was sixteen, then had a Mirena IUD for a year and a half. I didn't know what a normal cycle would be for me or how long it would take us to conceive.

Approximately eight weeks later, I didn't feel like myself and took a pregnancy test. This was the first and last time I looked at a negative pregnancy test as if it was no big deal and went on with my day. A couple days later, I woke up feeling sick and tested again. Two little pink lines appeared!

This was a healthy pregnancy, and my first baby is now five and a half years old.

I chose to replace the Mirena IUD at my six weeks postpartum appointment.

When our first baby turned seventeen months, we decided it was time to try for baby number two.

In September, I had my second Mirena IUD removed. We got pregnant easily the first time, so it will happen easily the second time, right? Wrong! I was just beginning the most debilitating journey of my life, and I didn't know it yet.

I started tracking my cycles and was ovulating around days 21-23 of my cycle, just like I had before.

We got a positive pregnancy test in November; I was surprised it happened so quickly. However, I tested again a few days after, and the line was faint. I started bleeding, and the line faded away.

To help you understand my story, I need to flash back to June of 2017. I had a UTI that month, which was odd for me. I hardly ever got them. I was treated with antibiotics; then, a week later, the symptoms came back. I went back to the doctor, and she said, "You don't have a UTI."

I said I felt the exact same and asked her, "How can that be?"

She took a culture, and nothing grew, so I wasn't given an antibiotic. I had the burning symptoms of a UTI but not consistently. I kept going back to my gynecologist, telling her I didn't feel right, but the culture never grew bacteria, so I was left to deal with the symptoms.

TIP: It's important to find a doctor who looks at your story individually, a doctor who believes the answer may be beyond what is common. Seek another opinion. Research everything you can and write down your questions. Reach out to other women in infertility groups who may be able to offer you advice or have a similar story.

After the chemical pregnancy, I wondered about the burning symptoms. Could the miscarriage and these symptoms be related? My gynecologist strongly felt that the two were unrelated.

I asked her to test me for every STD and anything she could culture because I wanted to know what was causing the burning. Everything came back negative. The symptoms were so bad I was in and out of urgent care and the ER. As a last resort, I was given doxycycline to kill anything that was atypical. I got relief for a month or two, then the burning symptoms came back.

In April the next year, I still wasn't pregnant, so I went back to my gynecologist, feeling frustrated. She wouldn't refer me to a fertility specialist until after one year of trying to conceive.

I kept having the burning sensation, not just with urination but out of the blue. I was worried that the symptoms were related to not being able to conceive, especially since I didn't feel like this when trying for our first baby. My doctor said, "No, sounds like the bladder," and referred me to a urologist.

A month later, I had my first urologist appointment. *He didn't even examine me.* He speculated it was interstitial cystitis and gave me a diet to follow. The diet consisted of foods that I was already eating. I didn't believe the diet would help and scheduled a second opinion with another urogynecologist for July. I wanted a definite answer because *I knew* this was why we weren't able to conceive.

The second urogynecologist scheduled me for a bladder scope and collected urine directly from the bladder to have cultured. The results of the bladder scope were normal and not suggestive of interstitial cystitis. The urine culture also came back clean.

Here I sat, in pain with symptoms no one understood or cared to find a diagnosis for. Every time I felt the burning (which was every day), my gut was telling me this is the reason I wasn't conceiving.

The next month, I had a follow up with my OB/GYN, and she did a hysterosalpingogram to make sure my tubes were open. The results were normal.

Our next step was for my husband to have a semen analysis. He had great results other than sperm morphology which came back with a level of three. A healthy sperm morphology is a level of 4 to 14. The REI said most fertile is 7 and above.

My gynecologist consulted with a reproductive endocrinologist specializing in infertility (REI). She was going to prescribe me Clomid; however, after talking to the REI, she wanted us to meet with him due to my husband's low morphology. I was hopeful. This is the solution I had been waiting for! (Nope, wrong again).

Our first appointment with the REI was scheduled for the end of October.

We continued trying conceive while waiting for our appointment with the REI; a couple weeks after the hysterosalpingogram, I had another positive pregnancy test. I thought, "Look! We don't need to see a specialist after all!" (Nope, wrong again). I called my gynecologist immediately, so she could check progesterone and have my hCG levels checked. My progesterone was normal, and my hCG was 25. This showed a very low hCG. In non-pregnant females the normal level is less than 5. Then, I started bleeding. Another early pregnancy loss. There's quite a range in what's considered normal depending on how far along a pregnancy is and how the number rises as the pregnancy progresses. My hCG would reach around 25 then I would miscarry. This showed I was having miscarriages shortly after implantation.

We went to meet with the REI.

The REI said I need something to regulate ovulation and recommended IUI. I told him about the symptoms of burning I had off and on and how I didn't have them when I conceived my daughter or any other time in my life. The REI blew it off and said it's not related.

He ordered a ton of bloodwork, and I had about twenty tubes of blood drawn. Shortly after meeting with the REI, I had another positive pregnancy test. It was the weekend, and I called the fertility office. They said they would see me Monday. Of course, Monday was too late. I watched the line fade away, and I started to bleed. This was my third miscarriage.

In January 2019, our IUI journey began.

> *TIP: Before you start IUIs, make sure to have everything investigated. I thought all lab work and testing would automatically be in place, but it's not.*

I was excited to have our first IUI; my husband was nervous. I felt like this was going to increase our chances so much! I started with a low dose of Letrozole. My body handled it well. When I went in for my first follicle check by ultrasound, I had good follicle growth and was approaching ovulation. Since I'm an ultrasound technician specializing in OB/GYN care, I was able to read my results as they were scanning me.

The REI and nurse practitioner recommended doing an Ovidrel injection the next day and a booster five days later due to my history of early miscarriages. They said the hormones from the Ovidrel shot have been shown to help prevent early miscarriage.. The first IUI was unsuccessful.

I changed gynecologists because the burning was getting worse. The doctor I switched to had experience working in infertility. I told him my story. He examined me and told me I had bacterial vaginosis and prescribed me antibiotics. I had never been diagnosed with bacterial vaginosis, so this was new to me.

We had two more unsuccessful IUIs. Each IUI, they increased my Letrozole, and I had great follicle growth.

The fertility office realized at this point that they had not completed lab work to check for natural killer cell elevation. The test did show an elevated level of these cells. This meant my body was in fight mode and could recognize a pregnancy as foreign and attack it to prevent implantation or cause miscarriage. For this reason, they prescribed a steroid I would take during ovulation and the two week wait to suppress the natural killer cells. They told me I could do a couple more IUIs with the steroid on board.

The REI also recommended my husband have a DNA fragment test done. His result was 25. Normal is under 20; abnormal is over 30. My new gynecologist referred my husband to a male infertility specialist who started my husband on a very low dose of Clomid because his testosterone was slightly low. He also told us he sees patients conceive with a DNA fragment result of 25 all the time.

After the third IUI with my fertility doctor, I noticed my endometrium was not thickening. My lining was 6mm at ovulation. I told the doctor I was worried about this. He said it "meets criteria." From my knowledge, it needs to be 8-10mm-plus for implantation. (This time, I was right).

TIP: BEFORE an IUI procedure, ask what transfer standards are and what the procedure is if you don't meet criteria on transfer day.

We completed the fourth and fifth IUIs. Same story, same result. Each IUI, my Letrozole was increased. My endometrium measured 6mm for both, and both IUIs were unsuccessful.

My lining was not getting thicker.

During the sixth cycle, my lining was 5mm nearing the time of ovulation. I said, "I'm not doing an IUI." They gave me Estrace to try to thicken my lining. It didn't work well, and nothing happened with that cycle.

I took a month off and made an appointment with a different REI for a second opinion for September.

At the end of August, I had my last appointment with our current REI. He said all they could offer me was IVF and recommended IVF with ICSI. I felt defeated. IVF was not an option for us. Knowing we conceived our first baby naturally; I didn't believe him. I knew they were missing something. I was determined to find it.

> *TIP: Advocate for yourself and research treatment options. Many doctors will stick to what's common and what works for most. Most is not everyone. I saw another infertility warrior's post about what she was diagnosed with, and it was the answer that changed everything for me.*

I returned to my OB/GYN because the burning was back. He tested for bacterial vaginosis and said there were very few cells. He upped my probiotics, hoping that would help. The burning would come and go and was slight. I had none of the other symptoms of bacterial vaginosis, just burning that never completely went away.

A month later, we met with a new REI. I am SO thankful we got this second opinion. He reviewed all my ultrasound images and labs. He said my lining was **too thin for any of these IUIs** and he wouldn't have done any of them, outside of the first. He said it was from the Letrozole, and the only change was to increase the Letrozole which, in turn, was making my lining worse.

> *TIP: When I asked about my endometrial lining being too thin, their response was that they saw women with that thickness of lining conceive. What's important is it wasn't working for me. The REI never changed protocol. They kept doing the same thing. They were increasing a medication that was causing ME a problem. I encourage you to ask for a tweak in protocol. What may work for the majority may not work for you. Investigate the medications being used. Research common side effects that could be working against you. Unfortunately, we did not do this.*

He said the big picture is I wasn't ovulating regularly and my lining was too thin. He didn't want to give me Clomid because it would do the same thing to my lining. Basically, I was ovulating so quickly with Letrozole that my lining didn't have time to thicken when the Letrozole was stopped.

> *TIP: Understand that if your lining is too thin or if your ovulation is too early, you can't conceive. The way the REI explained it was Letrozole keeps your lining thin to feed the follicles. Then, when the Letrozole stops, the lining starts to thicken. The Letrozole was causing me to ovulate too soon, so my lining hadn't had time to thicken once the Letrozole was stopped. This is commonly seen with Clomid, but Letrozole can do the same thing.*

The REI said there's one more medication we could try, tamoxifen. It works great for ovulation, and it also thickens the lining. We decided to do a couple cycles of "tamoxifen only" before going back to IUIs.

Like with Letrozole, I took tamoxifen during cycle days 3-7. I went in for a follicle scan a week later, and he wasn't happy with my lining. He said he wanted to check it during ovulation, which no one did before. He wanted me to do Ovidrel and come back right after ovulation. My lining was 8mm. He thought with another cycle of tamoxifen, my lining would start getting better.

The next month, I needed a break, so my REI let me take tamoxifen only. My lining was improving. In the meantime, I was doing a ton of research about my burning symptoms and why they never completely went away. Researching "bacteria" on an infertility support page, I came across an infection called ureaplasma. Lots of women were writing, "They don't check for this unless you ask," "I had it and got treated and got pregnant."

I researched urea plasma. I came across an article entitled "Ureaplasma, the treatable infection the infertility industry doesn't want you to know you have." I read the paper, crying. I felt like I wrote the paper; her symptoms and her journey were the same as mine.

Ureaplasma is a type of mycoplasma infection. It can start from a UTI and get in the reproductive tract; the symptoms are burning and bacterial vaginosis. I had my answer. I knew at that moment this was it, and I was going to fight to be heard until someone treated me for it.

TIP: I was told "no" by many physicians. I was told bacterial vaginosis and ureaplasma don't affect infertility. Each time, I would get madder and more frustrated. Each time a doctor told me "No," I moved on to the next. Find one who believes the patient is always right.

I called my OB/GYN and shared the information with him. He said I'd need to have the special test done called the **post coital test**. It needed to be done at ovulation within four hours of having intercourse. He said it is something that he **routinely tests his new patients for**, but I wasn't seeing him when I started my journey.

TIP: You MUST ask for the post coital test before IUI to save yourself so much heartache.

A skilled professional can see the sperm under a microscope and understand how they're traveling through the cervical mucus at the time of ovulation. My fabulous doctor saw that the sperm were not knowing where to go and were moving slowly, almost like they were sick. My mucus had tons of white blood cells due to the infection, making it hard for the sperm to travel to the egg. He prescribed an antibiotic for both my husband and me. (It is KEY to get your partner treated, too.)

He said with IUI, you are bypassing the cervical mucus. However, if I had it, my husband would, too. It can cause the sperm to be sick, not swim well, and not be able to fertilize the egg. I had two strikes against me during IUI – the ureaplasma and my lining being thin.

Both my first gynecologist and my REI missed testing me for this. I asked myself why wasn't this in place as a routine test? Many fertility offices skip this step because they either don't believe in the test, don't understand the test, or the test doesn't "pay the bills." Had I believed any of that, I never would have had more children.

I scheduled the post coital test for my next cycle then called my REI. I told them my symptoms and that I was worried about ureaplasma. They called me in the antibiotic azithromycin, a $10 antibiotic. They said it's extremely hard to grow ureaplasma on culture and can take several months ... if it ever grows. So, if it's suspected, they just start treatment.

The time of my post coital test arrived. My gynecologist said I had great cervical mucus, but he saw a lot of white blood cells. This indicates a mycoplasma infection. *Fertility offices don't check for this unless you ask. Many won't test you for it even if you ask. They disregard it and say it doesn't affect fertility. Here's the thing, ureaplasma is a normal bacteria in the body, but when it gets in the genital tract, it causes havoc.*

> *TIP: If you're seeing an OB/GYN, ask them to test you for this before investing in ANY procedure to avoid wasting time and money and causing heartache.*

Most women don't know they have ureaplasma, and *their only symptom is commonly infertility*. Often, they end up giving up before finding out they have it. The OB/GYN said the sperm can't travel through the mucus because it makes the mucus too thick. The sperm become sick and can't travel to the egg.

I was excited but also infuriated! I felt sick. I thought about all of the women who didn't have a miracle doctor to help them. Thankfully, I had symptoms. The urea plasma was causing bacterial vaginosis, so I had burning, which was my body's way of telling me something was wrong. **Remember, most women only have the symptom of infertility.**

> *TIP: Consult your doctor if you suspect ureaplasma. This was my treatment plan. My husband and I had a round of azithromycin a week before ovulation. (If that hadn't worked, we would have then been treated with doxycycline.) Then, I kept taking the azithromycin for a couple weeks after ovulation.*

Impatient to know my results early, I routinely test for pregnancy when the end of the two-week wait was nearing. Nine days post ovulation, I took a pregnancy test, not expecting to be pregnant. I had a faint line! I was cautious. Would the line stay? I immediately called my REI. I went in for progesterone and hCG lab work. My progesterone was 40, and my hCG was 10. The faint line never faded. We had our miracle! She's now 17 months old.

The cycle after our antibiotic treatment is the cycle we conceived. That cycle, I also ovulated on day 13 with tamoxifen, which was really good for me, and we skipped Ovidrel.

I'll never know for sure if the antibiotic cleared things up or it was just our time. A month before our positive test, I changed my prayers. I started praying for God to teach me how to let this all go to show me how to be okay with not having a second child. I knew that, for my health, I needed to give up, but I couldn't do it on my own. I was mentally unhealthy, out of money, and out of vacation time from work. I couldn't handle another failed IUI.

> *TIP: If your gut is telling you something isn't right ... run to a second opinion. Don't run away from infertility; run to a second opinion or a third opinion. It took me going through several doctors to find ones who would listen and help us to our miracle baby.*

When I thought our family would be a family of three, we were becoming a family of five. God wasn't telling me "No." He was telling me "Not yet."

I recently delivered another miracle! We conceived our third daughter while I was exclusively breastfeeding my second baby who was eight months old. No appointment, no needles, no doctors, no stress, no negative pregnancy tests, and no antibiotics. Looks like infertility was not the issue. Ureaplasma was.

Looking back now, I can't imagine life without my two youngest children. Had I listened to my first doctors, I would've given up, and these children wouldn't be here. IVF was never an option for us due to cost. When we thought a second baby was unimaginable, we were blessed with a second and then a third baby.

I heard about ureaplasma from another infertility warrior. If she hadn't talked about it, I wouldn't have known and wouldn't have fought to find someone to test me or treat me. I always tell people that while it was an absolutely debilitating journey, my two youngest wouldn't be who they are if there wasn't a wait, if there wasn't a heartache.

They healed my heart from the wrath of infertility. To know that overlooking ureaplasma and a ten-dollar antibiotic could have prevented them from being in my life is absurd. When I longed for a sibling for my oldest child and was ready to give up, there was a greater plan. I knew I had to fight for an answer. I had to fight for the two babies I hadn't met yet.

The love of a child is worth it. Don't give up. It's coming. I know it's a wicked twisted journey. One day, you will tell your story of how you overcame what you went through, and it will become someone else's survival guide.

MORE STORIES OF HELP AND HOPE FOR YOUR JOURNEY

Unlock a special video message from Erin and receive a free gift when you scan this code!

Erin is a girl mom of three who defeated secondary infertility twice. Her daughters are her inspiration to share her story. She will tell you being a mother is the greatest blessing of her life and her goal is to raise her girls to be best friends. She will also say to be your own advocate and to not take unexplained as an answer.

She's a dog mom, her dogs helped her through the hardest years of her life. Boxers have her heart.

Erin works part time as a high risk obstetrical medical Sonographer with 12 years of experience. She also works part time doing photography for children, infants, and families. Both careers are a passion involving capturing special moments of life.

Erin loves spending time at the lake in a small quaint country town with her family and friends.

She's always willing to share her journey as it could become someone else's survival guide.

IT'S A JOURNEY, HOLD ON (TO HOPE)

Wendy Vermaak

Similar to many of you reading this book, I am a type A personality. More accurately, I'm a triple type A with an A+ distinction. I like to plan and be in control. My struggle with infertility has graciously brought me down to size in realizing what I, apparently, cannot control. I was blissfully unaware of the journey ahead of me when I met the love of my life at 21 years old, got engaged at 22, and married at 23. We were young and healthy and wanted to wait a few years before starting a family. So determined was I in my planning that I made a gynae appointment just before getting married to be issued a prescription for the contraceptive pill and to make sure everything was okay 'down there.'

A few years later, at 26 years old, and according to my master plan, we decided it was time to start our family. In September, 2006 we went on European and UK Contiki tours back-to-back. I stopped taking the pill just beforehand so that we could fall pregnant on our first ever fun-filled overseas trip. How sweet. How naïve. I was surprised and irritated that my master plan of control and planning was thwarted.

A year later and after about 50 negative home pregnancy tests, frustrated and concerned, I visited my gynae. Gratefully, she referred us to a fertility clinic and fertility specialist immediately. I was so frustrated to have to wait 8 more weeks for this appointment. I mean, I was already way off my timeline schedule of having two kids by age 30.

While waiting for this appointment, my husband and I decided that IVF was not going to be part of our journey. Whilst we both have massive respect and awe for fertility treatment and the advancements that have occurred, we both strongly felt that IVF was not the way God was going to bless us. After a few visits with the amazing fertility specialist Dr. G., we quickly progressed through a myriad of tests, including blood tests, scans every 2 days, and sperm analysis. It felt like every test presented a new challenge and diagnosis – hormone imbalances, low AMH, PCOS, chocolate cysts, and abnormal sperm count, morphology and motility issues.

> *TIP: Don't delay in seeking specialized help from a fertility specialist. Don't waste any precious time.*

Whilst I was devastated on hearing that there was male factor infertility as well as my diagnosis, it did ease my guilt of being the ONLY one at fault. One of the routine tests was a post-coital test. This most undignified test is where the fertility specialist asks you to come in an hour or two after sex with your husband, so they can syringe out the gooey bits and slap them on a microscope. This was to check the secretions and performance of sperm under microscopic view. I remember being mildly worried that this was a step in the wrong direction from actually conceiving that month since they were taking swimmers out instead of leaving them in.

What this test revealed was that my husband's swimmers were actually fine, but I was now also dubbed as 'the sperminator' whose area 'down there' presented a hostile environment. So, it now *was* actually all my fault. I sobbed.

Unbelievably, as this test is performed during the same time as ovulation, and even though I had been renamed 'the sperminator,' I fell pregnant. Ha! Take that, medical science and scrutiny!

> *TIP: You are not "your diagnosis," and everyone is different. The doctors can only go by what they know and what is presented in front of them at the time. Try to not take every value, reading, or diagnosis as the final blow. Things can change. Things can be treated.*

Unfortunately, we had a miscarriage a few weeks later. We were devastated. I thought God had answered our prayers and was telling us that we were not going to need *too much* medical intervention. Following this, we had many more timed cycles, trigger shots, hormone injections, scans, and dwindling finances over a 6-year period.

Eventually, it was suggested we do an HSG. Obviously, being a triple type A, I researched this procedure extensively. On arriving for the procedure, I was eagerly expecting my mild sedative and a quiet, quick procedure that would rule out any more issues, and of course, I was likely to fall pregnant straight afterwards since the procedure and dye sometimes "flushes out your system." That was what the internet told me. It lied. There was no such sedation for South African women. Luckily for me, it was only mildly uncomfortable and followed by some awful cramping, not unlike my usual monthly menstrual cramps.

During the procedure, I could tell by the doctor's and nurse's faces that all was not well. Alas, there were no two blue lines on my home pregnancy test after that either.

At the follow-up appointment, I was informed that I had a probable septum creating an arcuate uterus, and this was possibly hindering conception or leading to miscarriages. This septum, or wall, had pulled my uterus into a heart shape. The recommendation for a laparoscopy and hysteroscopy was made to cut out the septum and explore and treat the possible endometriosis.

I was looking forward to the surgery as it seemed to be the biggest barrier, and I wanted it out of the way ASAP. After the surgery, with the septum removed and stage 3 endometriosis mostly obliterated, I had renewed hope. Wouldn't you believe it, a month later, we were pregnant again *without any medical assistance?*

Cautiously optimistic, we made it to the 6-week scan. Rejoice! There was a healthy heartbeat! At 10 weeks, though, we lost this baby, too. Yet again, we were crushed, and our hopes dashed. There wasn't any additional testing done to find out why we had another loss, and I was too devastated to even consider finding out if there were chromosomal problems. Added to this came further diagnoses cropping up of hormonal imbalances, low iron counts, and anovulation.

After about 5 years of this rollercoaster, I was blessed to find an in-person fertility support group. Kirsten, who founded this group, and many others in it were such an inspiration and support to me. To find that I was not alone and could cry, vent, and be understood was a true godsend. I learned so much from these strong, persevering women. There is something special about hearing a story face-to-face and first-hand, sinking into a couch and crying together – guttural, ugly, snotty cries, and hugs, love, and encouragement. These women will never know their impact on my life and how many hours of prayer were spent for them.

In these five years, over and above the medical fertility treatments, I also did everything I had heard about in this group that was available to me to help improve my chances of conceiving. I cut out all alcohol, switched to decaffeinated coffee, changed my diet to eat mostly fresh foods and a lot of fruits and vegetables that resembled the uterus and ovaries, (such as pears, avocados, and pomegranates), reflexology, acupuncture, chiropractic treatment, reduced my exercise regime to only moderate intensity, cranio-sacral therapy, body-stress release therapy, colour therapy, and Body Talk, vast amounts of counseling, bicarbonate of soda vaginal douches (for my hostile environment 'down there'), homeopathy, Chinese medicine consisting of vile tonics and tissue salts, fertility 'teas' and millions of supplements, as well as drinking from the same cup/glass as my pregnant friends (you know, just in case). Can you tell I was desperate?

Whilst none of these led to an actual full-term pregnancy and baby of our own, they did help with firstly meeting my *need* to be in control and feeling empowered, as well as offering some physical and psychological benefits. So, when a well-meaning 'fertile' friend, colleague, or family member offered some advice about 'Have you tried …. a/b/c?' or offered the inevitable but useless advice of 'just relax' or 'just adopt' or 'go on a holiday/get drunk/forget about it,' I could always retort that, YES I had already exhausted all those options.

TIP: Arm yourself with as much information as possible so that you can prepare well to support any fertility treatment you are undergoing. There are various supportive

> *treatments that might affect your overall mental and physical wellbeing that could enhance your ability to conceive.*

Interestingly, after 5 years of testing and stop-start treatment at the fertility clinic, IVF was never suggested as a next step intervention. In hindsight, that was rather strange for a fertility clinic, but I think it was God's hand in closing that door to us. Aside from the trauma and grind of the fertility journey, life also had its own challenges, including my father's traumatic death (with an unclosed murder case and investigation), my husband having several near-death experiences, marital challenges, having been held up at gunpoint, and my mother and step-father's very traumatic home invasion and beating.

> *TIP: During this all-consuming fertility journey, life's ups and downs happen. Seek support or counseling to deal with any additional traumas or stresses.*

During my prayer time, I especially prayed against receiving false prophecies. I knew I could not deal with a flippant comment from someone that 'of course' we would have a baby. My emotions were just too raw and vulnerable to tolerate that. By God's grace, I only received two prophecies that we would have a baby. One was from my husband's aunt, a truly God-anointed woman, who phoned me out of the blue and told me to buy a baby onesie. I thanked her but didn't truly believe, after all we had been through, that this hope could be for me. Then, my husband also announced a few months later that he was sure we were going to be pregnant by the end of that same year. They were right!

With God's mercy and grace, we received the blessing of a healthy baby boy after 7 years TTC and without any medical intervention. After a rocky NICU start, the next 18 months with our healthy miracle baby boy were utter bliss. We restarted the TTC journey with renewed hope. Our previous TTC traumas were no longer top of mind, and we conceived again with minimal effort.

We were elated and relieved at not having to go through the same distress as before in trying to conceive. But at 9 weeks, we had another miscarriage. I was not prepared for the grief this brought. All the past hurts and traumas came back in an all-consuming flood. I decided to allow nature to take its course and for the pregnancy to 'come away' on its own. This was over a Christmas period, and I felt like a walking tomb for over 2 weeks, carrying my dead baby.

The psychological trauma of that hollowed me out completely. I eventually requested the suggested D&C, which turned out to be another disaster. Having to fill out the hospital form 'Are you pregnant?' nearly tipped me over the edge. What insanity is it to have this on that hospital form for a woman who has miscarried?

Another 2 years went by of actively trying. During this time, we had the added questions and tears from a toddler asking and praying each night for a sibling. This was gut-wrenching. In a way, I didn't consider that secondary infertility could be as painful as it was. I now felt I was not only failing my husband, but also my miracle child. My health seemed to be on the decline with unexplained severe fatigue, hair loss, and body aches. After a number of specialist physician visits and blood tests, I was diagnosed with Hashimoto's disease. After that diagnosis and treatment, we had another miracle conception and yet another miscarriage. There really aren't words to describe this level of disappointment and lost hope, AGAIN. We were absolutely spent. In every way.

By this time, I had now become one of several women who headed up the original fertility support group. I was happily able to pour myself into that and to support and encourage others but was unable to be hopeful for myself.

> *TIP: Find real support from those who are more than just nosy. Be choosy about what you share and with whom, as not everyone 'has your back,' understands your pain or choices, or perhaps truly supports you, but rather judges.*

I also began pouring my life into many 'compensatory' situations, somehow bargaining with God and myself to find a way to be part of pregnancy journeys and successes. I planned and hosted a number of baby showers, bought many cute over-the-top baby gifts, taught pregnant women's exercise classes for many years, and continued to volunteer at a girls' home for teenage pregnant girls. The desire to be a family of four never left my heart, but Jesus graciously and gently slowly removed my desire for *striving* for one. On turning 40 in 2020, I decided to really celebrate and to take a break from striving, even with yearning, after 14 years TTC.

I was still active in the fertility support group but in a very different way. Since the Covid-19 pandemic halted our face-to-face meetings, we kept to virtual meetings and stayed in touch via social media.

> *TIP: Don't forget to actually live your life whilst in the 'wait' for your blessing. Time will pass anyway, so try to fill your time with attainable but challenging goals and meaning.*

After initiating a specific calling to be especially prayerful and involved with some of the support group ladies still struggling to conceive, I was blessed with another natural conception. My husband and I were absolutely ecstatic. Initially, this was still somewhat fraught with anxiety after all the previous losses. Adding to the stress, I was diagnosed with COVID-19 literally 24 hours after finding out I was pregnant. It was clear that I had very little control other than looking after my general health as much as possible. With close monitoring from my family doctor and my gynae, we slowly made it to each checkup and scan, anxious with anticipation of seeing that miraculous heartbeat, appropriate growth, and the screening necessary for all the geriatric pregnancy requirements to check for chromosomal issues or abnormalities. Each week brought some relief and building excitement. The greatness of this blessing was never taken for granted, and much prayer and care surrounded protecting myself and this pregnancy as far as was possible. With great praise and thanks to God, at 42 years old, we welcomed our second son in March 2022, and almost 9 years after welcoming our first miracle son. This was an almost 16-year journey to be my heart's desire, a 'family of four.'

I believe my infertility journey has shaped me to be a more tolerant and patient mother and am certain it will be the same for you. When one has been desperate for so long, the pregnancy niggles are better tolerated, the night-time feeds, fatigue, and childhood illnesses are better managed. You are being refined right now to be the best mother you can be. Hold onto hope and know that I'm already praying for you.

Unlock a special video message from Wendy and receive a free gift when you scan this code!

Wendy is a wife, mom and biokineticist by profession (exercise rehabilitation specialist) in private practice. She is actively involved in running a face-to-face fertility support group for those TTC, as well as involved in various ministry projects. She has also served on the Biokinetics Association of South Africa board of directors for over 5 years, as well as a volunteer and board director for Health Care Matters, an NPO, providing pro bono treatment to disabled elderly people in a convalescent home and young pregnant teenage girls at a girls home. Wendy has also had ample lecturing experience lecturing clinical exercise science and pathophysiology at the University of Johannesburg.

Wendy has a passion for supporting and encouraging women on the fertility journey, whether it be for practical advice, a listening ear, or a chance to offer a cup of coffee, a tissue, and some compassion.

I DISAGREE

Dr. Patrick and Christy Flynn

Everyone has a story – every demographic and every walk of life. Regardless of who or what or when, what is common to all of us is that we each *have a story*. Each story is unique, and each story is important. They shape who we are and who we become. Collectively, our stories impact what happens in our generation and for generations to come.

As you go through the journey of your life, your story, you encounter circumstances and situations that change you. It's part of the process and essential in determining how you think and look at the world. It can happen directly or indirectly – sometimes, you learn from things you go through yourself, and other times, the experiences of others can have a tremendous effect.

I'm going to share pieces of my story that have laid the groundwork for our family's legacy. Some parts may seem distant to you, while others may resonate so strongly that you see yourself in the scene. I have learned from things I've gone through myself, as well as things I've watched others experience. It has all led to thinking in a way that has empowered me and others to make lasting changes in their story – changes that seemed impossible, changes for the good.

> *Tip: Many people see fertility as it affects the woman who so desperately wants to become a mother. In reality, it can affect men and their hopes and dreams as well. Remembering to support both, the man and the woman, is imperative.*

My story started when I met a girl that I fell in love with, and I fell hard! We knew mutual acquaintances who had tried to set us up on blind dates months before, but we had both bailed. I was busy with school, or at least, that was my excuse. But 19 years ago, God orchestrated a chain of events that changed my life forever. I will never forget the day I met her.

During the summer, I was a water skier for a show ski team from my hometown of Crivitz. One day, the pyramid fell on me, and I gashed my cheek. I also had a mild concussion, so I went to get adjusted by a chiropractic buddy I used to intern with. While I was there, a beautiful young lady with blond hair, short shorts, long legs, and platform heels came in without an appointment. We were introduced and hit it off immediately! I later learned this was the SAME girl I was set up on blind dates with, the ones we had both bailed on. (Crazy, right?)

Two days later, we started dating. No joke! She told me, "I'm going to marry you someday," and I told her, "You're right!" There was something amazing and unique about this girl. We spent the first couple weeks of our relationship sharing our hearts and what we each wanted for our lives. She shared her dreams; I shared my vision and direction for my life. We discussed the family we wanted to have, where we wanted to live, our passions, and our goals. We also shared how we would raise our children and how we wanted to make a difference in the world. Remember, we were young. My career was just getting started. We had the whole world ahead of us.

Two weeks into our relationship, I went to her house, excited to see the beautiful woman I had fallen in love with. When I got there, she was sobbing and in pain. This wouldn't be the last time I would find her like this. I often found her on the floor in the coming months, curled up in pain. It crushed me to see her like this. I wanted to know what I could do to help.

I would do anything for her. This wasn't just any girl – this was THE girl! So … why was she sobbing? I thought things were going so well. It turned out she had gotten her period that day, leaving her crying and in tremendous pain. She was always so happy; I had no idea she had so much pain in her life.

There was more to this story than just female problems or hormone issues. In order to understand the bigger picture of what was really happening, let's step back a bit and look at Christy's life and health history.

Christy had struggled most of her life with various illnesses and conditions, and they got progressively worse as she entered college. Years later, she told me that before we met, she had never pictured her life past the age of 25. That's how sick she was.

> *Tip: If you can't imagine life beyond a certain point, you need to find a new doctor. Christy was on the right track by seeing different specialists. The problem was they all thought along the same lines. She needed a different perspective.*

Christy's Thoughts: What was I thinking that day when Patrick found me sobbing and in pain?

Why would a guy like him – someone so confident, bold, and driven to achieve his future goals and dreams – want to be with a girl like me? You see, I was sick and had had many health challenges throughout my life up to that point. We had already talked about what we dreamed our futures would look like. I honestly didn't know what my future would look like because doctors had given me a grim outlook. I had excruciating GI issues, including ulcerative colitis, on the road to becoming Crohn's. The medical doctor's best advice at the time was, "drink Maalox before and after every meal." Seriously? I did that, and I was so much worse! All they could offer me were more drugs, and later on, surgery would be inevitable. To me, that was crazy!

Around that same time (while I was in college), my reproductive issues also began taking over my life. From migraines to incredible cramping, I felt like every organ of my body was slowly shutting down. The doctors and specialists monitored my symptoms and then suggested drugs. I refused the drugs, so they insisted on monitoring me monthly with ultrasounds. They confirmed that I had cysts on my ovaries and endometriosis. They told me I would probably not be able to bear children, or if I were to conceive, I would not be able to carry the pregnancy to term. Then, they graciously offered to scrape my uterus. I politely said, "No, thank you," and never returned to that office again. My mom had shared other details of my health history, and as a result, I was at peace with the fact

> *that I might not be able to bear my own children. I could definitely adopt someday.*

So, getting back to this pivotal, emotional moment in our lives, Christy began to share with me for the first time the health struggles that she had endured. I was shocked that she was struggling like this; I had no idea. She even went so far as to say, "Maybe we shouldn't be together." Now, I had a decision to make. While we had been sharing our hearts in that fantastic first two weeks of our relationship, I had shared with her that I wanted a big family.

So, I had a choice to make right then and there. Do I stay with her, or do I leave her? I'm not kidding when I told you I had completely fallen head over heels for that beautiful woman. Do I chalk this up as a setback? Or do I choose to use it as a setup for one of the greatest gifts God has ever given me?

Because I loved Christy and we had a future in front of us that we both clearly wanted, the choice was obvious. The choice was her; it was us. It was easy to choose us because I had fallen madly in love. She asked, "But what about your dream of having children? The doctors say I might never be able to give you a child."

When I looked at that beautiful woman I loved, I realized that two words would define our future. *I disagree.* I disagreed with every doctor she saw. I disagreed with the general practitioners. I disagreed with the gynecologists. I disagreed with the specialists. I even disagreed with the chiropractor, who was giving her regular adjustments and great supplements. The beautiful woman I fell in love with was meant to have children just like every other woman. There was something they were all missing. I didn't know what it was, but I was determined to find out.

> *Tip: The body doesn't make mistakes. It adapts. Figuring out why Christy's body was adapting in these specific ways would give me insights into what was going on to cause her these challenges.*

I engulfed myself in the study of female hormones. I devoured everything I could find – every research article, every study, everything. I spoke with other doctors I respected, people who had been my instructors while I was in school and others who had a mindset to look at things differently than the doctors who were giving her no hope. I wanted to see multiple perspectives and put the pieces together. I studied female hormones like a fanatic.

The best answers I found were disheartening. All I could think was, *Man, this can't be all there is!* I knew this didn't line up with what I had been taught in school. I couldn't settle for what I was finding. I knew there was more to it. I had to keep digging and look at it from a different approach. I had to think differently.

Just because we have what appears to be a fairytale life doesn't mean it was easy. We had obstacles. Every decision you make will have obstacles. The question is will you overcome the obstacles to get to the end you want?

> *Christy's Thoughts: Some people say they wish they knew exactly what obstacles they would face in life so they could prepare. If I had known how hard my journey would be, I don't think I would've had enough courage to walk it out. By the grace of God, I was introduced to a man I fell in love with, and he turned my world upside down. For so long, I felt alone in my health journey. Appointment after appointment, I kept hearing the same two things:*

"We aren't sure why" and "here are some drugs and surgery to help your pain." I was discouraged to say the least – even a bit depressed at times.

The medical method was getting me nowhere, and I kept feeling worse. I couldn't eat typical healthy foods like salad, certain fruits, or vegetables, and I had been allergic to dairy since the second grade. I had been seen and referred to so many doctors, but no one could give any answers on how to become healthy. I was exhausted and ready to try something different.

So, imagine me on the floor crying, being vulnerable with Patrick for the first time. I was so afraid of what was going to come next. But then, he said something no one had ever said to me. "Don't worry about any of this. You're going to be okay." I chose at that very moment to trust him – a guy I had just met – with my health and future. How crazy is THAT?!?

I knew this road would be challenging to travel, but the medical model had nothing to offer me that made sense. I chose to trust the process of the journey we would be walking together.

I may have been a new doctor, but I was convinced a woman's body was meant to have babies. You see, I believe all bodies are created for homeostasis. *Homeostasis* is health and function. That was more than any other doctor had offered her. I chose to look at things differently and not settle for the answers she had been given. This unfamiliar approach was foreign to both of our families. As a result, it caused stress and struggles within our relationships. We chose to stay with it no matter what, including all the criticisms that come when living under a microscope.

What's the result? What was the impact of our decision to pursue Christy's health? We have four amazing daughters. Yes, I have FOUR daughters. You can please all pray for me now! I joke, but they are amazing and bring so much joy to our lives.

> *Tip: Any time you decide to go against the norm, you'll have obstacles and challenges. Some of the hardest will be with people you love, likely family and friends. You have to decide whether you will live in their expectations or take the path that is right for you.*

Sometimes, I wonder what my life would have been like if I hadn't chosen Christy. If we hadn't disagreed with what western medical thinking offered. I know it wouldn't be as amazing as life with Christy and these four girls.

There's another huge impact from that original choice to pursue a different understanding of health, one I hadn't known at the time when Christy and I chose to build a future together – a result impacting men, women, and children worldwide. It was a change of thought process. I had to look at things from a different perspective and not just settle for the "one size fits all" method the traditional medical world uses.

Now, others are learning to ask questions and think differently. That is a big deal for a culture that has historically never questioned anyone in a white coat; they are considered the experts. There is a lot of power in those two words, *I disagree*. More people are saying it because of the decisions my wife and I made over 23 years ago. If you think about it, that is a significant impact, much bigger than we could have imagined at that time.

> *Tip: Your very personal story may have a reaching impact. You may not see the "why" at the moment. Your perspective may be what it takes to help the next person.*

Actually, a huge national company impacting thousands of people a year from around the world would not exist if I hadn't chosen my wife. The Wellness Way wouldn't be where it is today if I hadn't chosen Christy and her unique health. This pivotal change of thought process impacted my wife and created the opportunity for us to have a family with those four amazing daughters. Now, I'm using our experience to help families all over the world. I'm here to empower you in your choices; they have an impact. My impact all started with a change in my thought process.

MORE STORIES OF HELP AND HOPE FOR YOUR JOURNEY

Unlock a special video message from Dr. Patrick and Christy and receive a free gift when you scan this code!

Dr. Flynn is a chiropractor and the founder of The Wellness Way clinics. As a young child, he was labeled as a troubled kid. He had a hard time learning, focusing, and existing in the school system, and he struggled with the larger world around him.

Years later, as a teenager, he went through a series of events that led him to figure out he had immune issues that caused him to experience neurological challenges. This discovery started Dr. Flynn on his journey, defining his purpose and initiating his pursuit of education, ultimately leading him to create a different approach in healthcare. He has attended numerous colleges and taken countless classes from learning institutions, all of which have resulted in him focusing on hormones and the immune system.

After 23 years, he has trained thousands of doctors, and his network has reached over 80 clinics worldwide. Dr. Flynn also has an international bestselling book "I Disagree: How These Two Words Are the Secret to Thinking Differently and Taking Control of Your Health," and a seminar for the public called "The Hormone Connection" that has been seen by hundreds of thousands of people around the world. Despite his numerous accomplishments, he still says he is just a small-town country boy who came up with an idea to help people.

Christy Flynn is a vital contributor to The Wellness Way. She partners with Dr. Patrick to ensure the message of hope and support for moms raising their children in a healthy lifestyle reaches those looking for it. With him since the beginning, she knows the challenges for women, and especially moms, to find the resources and support to live against the grain of the mainstream.

WHAT HAPPENS TO THE HEART?

Angela Kelleher

As one of eight children, with over 20 nieces and nephews, I was not expecting infertility to be part of my life journey. Two years of trying and five unsuccessful IUI attempts, my then-husband and I went for our first IVF treatment. The first few days were a breeze, and I clearly remember saying out loud to a friend that this was much easier than I expected. Then, day four happened. Wham, those hormones hit me like a punch in the face! I wanted to KILL. Someone. Anyone. Once the rage subsided, I wanted to slit my wrists. It did not help that my ovaries were not responding and producing a million eggs. I swung back to rage. I could have killed the next person who told me, "It only takes one."

The retrieval produced six gammy-looking eggs. But from the moment of fertilisation, I called the fertility lab every day to ask how they were doing and ask the team to remind those little embryos that we loved them already and to please hang on for us. We offered them virtual burgers and milkshakes – anything a potential child might want!

Those people were right – it only took one. One embryo made it and implanted beautifully. Welcome to my womb, little cherished one. My HCG levels climbed perfectly, and other than extreme exhaustion, I had nothing to complain about. I WAS PREGNANT! What could I complain about!?

By our six-week scan, that one had turned into two. Our precious embryo had split, and we were expecting identical twins. This apparently explained the exhaustion. We were elated, on cloud nine – what a surprise! Two tiny, precious babies. I immediately got to work finding breast feeding cushions to support feeding two babies at once. I drafted designs for a Noah's ark two-by-two-themed nursery. My friends bought me books on raising twins. It was a euphoric time.

Week seven, our fertility specialist said he needed to warn us how precarious an identical twin pregnancy can be. He went through a long list of problems that could arise. We heard words like monochorionic/diamniotic (Mo/Di), dichorionic/diamniotic (Di/Di), monoamniotic-monochorionic (MoMo), twin-to-twin transfusion (TTTS) syndrome and more. Honestly, it went in one ear and out the other. Nothing could dampen this honeymoon period. This was not going to happen to us. The nursery plans continued in earnest. These babies would know they were the most wanted and loved that any babies could be.

The weekly scans continued; our precious babies grew in size from a peppercorn to a pomegranate seed to a blueberry to a raspberry to a cherry. What a precious concept!

And then, just like that, the heavens came crashing down around us. It was not like a mild rain but with floods, storms, crashing thunder, and tsunamis. Our babies were in trouble.

First up came the news that ours was a monochorionic-diamniotic pregnancy. Mo/Di are identical twins who share a placenta but not an amniotic sac. Mo/Di twins have high rates of birth weight discordance, fetal growth restriction, and prematurity. One twin may fail to develop a proper heart and become dependent on the pumping activity of the other twin's heart, resulting in twin reversed arterial perfusion. If one twin dies in utero, blood accumulates in that twin's body, causing the death of the remaining twin. The risks are very high.

The news got worse. Our babies had twin-to-twin transfusion (TTTS). In simple terms, this means that their circulatory systems intermingle at random and create connections between the babies' blood vessels. This can cause a disproportionate blood supply aka TTTS. It occurs when blood moves from one twin to the other. The twin that loses the blood is called the donor twin. The twin that receives the blood is called the recipient twin. Both infants may have problems depending on the severity of the transfusion. The donor twin may have too little blood, and the other may have too much blood. The donor twin may need a blood transfusion, while the recipient twin may need to have the amount of blood in his or her body reduced. The donor twin is usually born smaller than the other twin, usually with paleness, anemia, and dehydration. The recipient twin is born larger, with redness, too much blood, and increased blood pressure. Because of the increased blood volume, the recipient twin may develop cardiac failure and also require medications to strengthen heart function.

If left untreated, the survival rate for TTTS twins is approximately 10 to 15 percent. To really pour salt on already devastating wounds, TTTS was untreatable in South Africa, where we were living. Our only glimmer of hope was to make it to 20 weeks of pregnancy, raise the funds, and then travel to Europe or the USA for treatment.

Armed with that glimmer, we set off on a fact-finding mission. Who could help us and how?

In the meantime, our fertility specialist organized an emergency appointment with a fetal specialist. This remarkably thorough and kind man first told us we were expecting boys but then delivered the devastating news that one of our boys had developed a condition called prune belly syndrome (PBS).

PBS is a rare, genetic, birth defect affecting about 1 in 40,000 births. About 97% of those affected are male. It is a congenital disorder of the urinary system and is a serious and often life-threatening problem. Most infants with prune belly syndrome are either stillborn or die within the first few weeks of life from severe lung or kidney problems. Our little boy's chance of survival was getting slimmer by the minute. And as a result, his brother was also at major risk because of the TTTS connection. *Have you ever heard a heart scream?* Mine was. But still, there was that little glimmer of hope – have laser surgery overseas at 20 weeks.

> *TIP: One step at a time. Sometimes, all we need is a glimpse of hope ... possibility ... to take that first or even final step.*

Following that appointment with the fetal specialist, we decided to name our boys – Ronan and Ruairc. Ronan on the right-hand side of my belly, Ruairc on the left. Ronan our little wise seal, Ruairc a judicious hero and leader. Both are strong names for young men in the making.

I spoke with world-renowned specialists from overseas. The little glimmer of hope we had was tinged with extreme sadness. Ronan would be born with major physical problems and would need comfort care until he died soon after birth. It is the saddest thing to imagine yourself as a new mom holding your dying baby, that they may not survive more than a few hours. Though he was fatally diagnosed, there was never a doubt in my mind regarding carrying him to term. My arms ached to hold that little baby tight and tell him how much I loved him.

We then made the terrible mistake of going to see another fetal specialist to try and get help locally. This brutal woman took one look at our boys and told us to immediately abort and move on quickly with another IVF cycle. We left her rooms broken. Even knowing I was carrying terminally diagnosed babies, termination was never for us.

At 16 weeks, we had our first appointment with our gynaecologist. This was the wonderful man who had helped us with our IUI treatments and insisted we waste no more time – we needed urgent intervention from a fertility specialist. I remember how sad he was that day as we filled him in on the missing bits of our pregnancy story. He began to perform our scan and have another listen to those beautiful heartbeats and see their little bodies developing. But there were no heartbeats from either of the boys. They were gone. Our gynaecologist hung his head and cried with us.

I was sent for an immediate D&C. Screaming and crying, I begged them to scan again in case there was a mistake. No mistake. My boys were dead. I begged to be allowed to hold them. More trauma – as they were so premature, they were considered hospital waste, and I was not allowed to see them or take their bodies for a memorial service. It felt like someone had cast a cruel spell over us. This could not possibly be real.

Tip: Every hospital is different. If YOU feel like you want or need closure by seeing, holding, or memorializing your child, make sure that you and your partner pursue every avenue

> *to make this happen. Lean on your partner to help you advocate for yourself.*
>
> *I needed hope that I could find hope, if that even makes sense. And that's what I want for you – to find hope again. But simultaneously, I want to validate your utterly and painfully broken heart.*

At home that night, I began a dangerous cycle of drinking wine to purge the pain. All I managed was to purge the contents of my stomach, night after night down the toilet bowl. The pain did not go away. I remember being at the grocery store one day a few weeks later and having a major anxiety attack. I was standing stock still in the middle of the store and wanted to scream at everyone, "How can you keep moving and living; don't you know my boys have died?" How is it the world still continued to move on though I was dead inside. I called my psychologist that day and admitted I wanted to die, too.

> *TIP: It doesn't matter when your loss occurred, whether it was an early miscarriage, or if you had the chance to spend a few moments with your baby before they died. Babies are not interchangeable, and any subsequent child born is not a replacement.*
>
> *If you are having thoughts like I was about dying, reach out to someone who cares about you for help. I would not be the person/mother I am today without the help I received after my boys passed on.*

Through intense psychological intervention and medication, I made it through and came out the other side a more jaded and hardened version of me. I read a book called *An Exact Replica of a Figment of My Imagination*. In her ninth month of pregnancy, the author Elizabeth McCracken learned that her baby boy had died. How do you deal with and recover from this kind of loss? You don't, but you go on. I went on. I got back to work. I smiled to mask the sadness. I spoke with my husband about doing another IVF cycle. I did all the normal stuff I was expected to do.

> *Insight:*
>
> *"A trend has set in where those in mourning are not only isolated but put on the clock. With a timer in one hand and a bouquet of flowers in the other, our culture looks down at the bereaved and says, 'It's ok that you're not ok... for now.' And the clock starts ticking." Still Standing Magazine*
>
> *My experience showed me exactly how true this is, and it still hits a nerve with me to this day. Grief has no timeline, don't ever let anyone make you feel otherwise!*

We did another IVF cycle. Our fertility specialist advised us to go straight for donor eggs as mine at that point were past their use-by date. But we did not listen. IVFs number two and three were a waste of time and money. They only succeeded in compounding my depression and caused huge weight gain.

> *TIP: For those who don't always get the good news, it takes a lot of everything to begin again. I had to find courage, money, strength, endurance, support, willpower and health. I had the fortune at this stage of having met a number of*

> *remarkable people trying to conceive, and their support was irreplaceable. Don't be afraid to rely on those around you. Find those people for yourself.*

For IVF number four, we knew it was donor eggs or nothing. So began the process of looking at hundreds of potential egg donor profiles. Hair colour, eye colour, weight, education – I had it all in a spreadsheet. Which lady would be the best fit? We found one we really liked. I Google stalked for days until I figured out who she was. Tall, fit, very sporty, gay, healthy, good career – she seemed perfect. But the donation agency wasn't. The woman who owned it offered us a two-thousand-rand discount if I met her at the mall with the other 11 thousand in cash in a bag. We declined the offer but went ahead with signing up this donor. That yielded six embryos; two were good enough for transfer but sadly did not implant. I am forever grateful to this lady, though, for trying to help us have our baby.

The whole experience with the agency owner had left a bad taste in our mouths, and we decided to try a different agency for our fifth IVF cycle. From the get-go, they were amazing. I was assigned a consultant who was both empathetic and professional. I knew we were in the right hands.

This time, instead of trawling through hundreds of potential donors, we were very specific about how we would find the right donor. I wanted a lady who had given birth herself and had participated in an egg donation that led to the live birth of the baby. We received a shortlist of eight women. All seemed excellent – how to choose now was the dilemma. Eventually, through the power of spreadsheets, we made it down to one. All the Google stalking in the world was to no avail; I never managed to track her down.

> *TIP: Donor conception is a blessing we are fortunate to have in this day and age. Regardless of needing a donor egg, I knew this baby would be mine from the minute he/she fertilised. I would love this baby with the fierce strength of a lioness. Always.*

Another six embryos. Two were of great quality, one mediocre, and three did not cut the grade. I insisted on putting all three back on transfer day. The third embryo was not good enough to freeze, and I was sure as hell not letting a potential baby go. Lucky number three it was, because one of those little embryos buried itself deep in my endometrial lining. My bum was bruised black from progesterone injections, and I bled for the first ten weeks. I held very little hope of this baby making it. But every week, we were stunned to see and hear this amazing little heartbeat.

At 13 weeks, we learned it was a little girl and were overjoyed. Because of our history, we had to see the fetal specialist twice. Both were amazingly positive appointments. Our baby girl was thriving. We moved back to our gynaecologist, who was as excited for us as we were. We named our precious little girl Saoirse Rose. Saoirse is Irish for freedom, and the name symbolized so much for us after this journey with infertility.

Our 20-week scan was perfect; Saoirse was perfect. We could let our breath go; I was safely pregnant. The chance of anything happening to this baby was slim, but still, I was treated as a high-risk pregnancy, thankfully. I ended up in hospital twice with preterm labour. That was a living nightmare. At 26 weeks, Saoirse was too small still to give birth to. Yet, she persevered.

Bizarrely I had found 'a sign' that I clung to. About halfway through the pregnancy, I re-read our donor's profile and noticed that her birth date was March 08, as was mine – and believe it or not, Saoirse's due date was also March 08. I took it as a sign from the universe. Despite always being anxious about her well-being, I loved being pregnant. It was a beautiful, serene time. Her new nursery reflected that. It was a place of perfection, just like our beautiful daughter.

> *TIP: Give yourself grace during a pregnancy after loss. Give yourself grace for the mess and the unknowns, and take this one day at a time. Fear may feel as if it abounds for now, but hold tight. There is joy and hope to be found here, too.*

Saoirse decided otherwise for her birth date and arrived into the world on February 20th in the early hours of the morning, much to the horror of my gynaecologist. He likely had a busy Friday planned, and there I was at home, parking off, enjoying the contractions and last kicks from inside. My waters broke as I entered the hospital, and I was rushed off for a c-section. Hearing those first cries as she entered the world was precious, watching her head emerge from my tummy was magical. Here she was, our tiny dreamed-of baby. I clung to her and cried. Our rainbow baby had arrived!

At this time of writing, Saoirse is now a nine year-old girl. She is a strong-willed and beautiful child, and I am grateful every day to have the honour of being her mother. Sadly, my marriage did not survive, but she is being raised by two parents who have the highest hopes of being the best role models they can be and are co-parenting as best as possible.

How am I now? Marginally whole. I say marginally as I don't think one can ever be whole again after such a traumatic journey. Or perhaps it would be better phrased as I am a new version of me, a damaged version of innocence lost. Broken dreams were replaced by new dreams. I am more empathic and tolerant, grateful for surviving.

I have a strong desire to help others but no need for recognition and glory.

It's a mostly good place. Saoirse makes it whole. But there are days when it hits me hard in the face/soul that my boys died. And so, tragedy and triumph learn to exist alike.

I write this story in honour of Saoirse Rose, Ronan and Ruairc, our egg donor, and all the wonderful people we met along our journey to becoming parents. I write this story for YOU, my new friend reading this. May you find solace and companionship in my words and the words of all the wonderful women contributing to this book.

INFERTILITY SUCCESS

Unlock a special video message from Angela.

Angela Kelleher grew up in Ireland, the seventh of eight children. Coming from fertile stock, she never expected infertility to be part of her journey. Over the course of the past 10 years, Angela has made it her mission to destigmatize infertility. With a career in marketing to aid her, Angela helped found and run an NGO dedicated to assisting people struggling with infertility. She has also worked for various international infertility clinics in educating patients and the medical community.

Having lived abroad for close to two decades, Angela recently returned to Ireland to raise her daughter. Together, they live with their two dogs, two cats, and whatever other little critters cross their path.

BY THE MOON AND THE STARS

Raylene de Villiers

I'm sitting in the waiting area. It's the office of a very expensive fertility doctor. "I really don't belong here," I think to myself. "It can't be that bad." My husband and I have been trying to conceive for about six months – not *that* long really.

Being the A-type personality I am, I made an appointment at one of the most successful fertility clinics in Johannesburg, South Africa. I have spent an inordinate amount of time on Google, trying to search for possible reasons why I am not pregnant yet. Could it be blocked tubes? Aging eggs (I'm 26 years old)? Poor sperm count? A wonky thyroid, maybe just bad luck …. the list is quite endless. My husband felt that I was being "ridiculous." He thought I should just chill on the baby front and enjoy the fun of making one. I should have listened to him, and retrospectively, I admit to learning a very hard lesson in patience.

The appointment was scheduled and then unexpectedly my husband had to travel abroad for business. I had already waited a few weeks for this appointment and was certainly not about to cancel or reschedule it. The fertility clinic is a two-hour round-trip journey from our home, so taking time off work was required. I took the morning off and went about the trip by myself, not quite knowing what I would find out. I expected a few blood tests, a few questions, maybe an explanation that would quell my scientific brain just a little.

I enter the fertility doctor's office and sit down with my graphs and cycle lengths and list of questions.

> *TIP: If you don't immediately hit it off with your fertility doctor, find a new one. You need that connection with someone whom you can trust and have a bond with because there will be some months that they see your lady bits more than your husband does.*

I really don't like him much, but my hope is pinned on him, so I listen. He asks me a few questions, one of them being, "Do you notice any hair growing out of your chin?" "Strange?" I think; what a random question to ask, especially because the answer is "yes"! He pops me up on the scanning table, inserts the wand, and proclaims that I have polycystic ovarian syndrome (PCOS).

Wait … what? I haven't Googled that one yet. He explains that my cycle lengths are long as my eggs take forever to mature and ovulate. He immediately writes out a prescription for some hormonal injections and tells me to return in two days to check if the eggs are growing. I haven't even discussed this with my husband, but I made the decision to go ahead, and before I know it, the clinic sister is injecting me with my very first taste of my life for the next five years. I leave the clinic ecstatic that I/we (see what I did there?) have a plan. There is hope after all!

> *TIP: Don't be bullied into a pace you are not comfortable with. Fertility specialists want to help get you pregnant ASAP, which is, of course, what I wanted too, BUT I feel I could have gone a bit more slowly at this stage. Being able to talk to my husband would have helped my emotions.*

And that, my friends, is the start of the end that leads us down the rabbit hole of infertility treatments. Many times, I felt just like Alice in Wonderland, getting sucked up and out, growing in hope and pride and then shrinking in defeat and shame.

My husband returns from his trip abroad to have a lab form thrust into his hands – he needs to urgently do a sperm test to decide if we are going to try naturally this round or try intrauterine insemination (IUI). My husband is far from impressed with me. The test reveals that my husband has a low sperm count, motility, and mobility. We did two rounds of IUI with no success.

Apparently, I respond beautifully and have a fair number of eggs on the sonar each time, but now, the sperm seem to be the issue. We take a handful of vitamins and supplements daily and have both started Chinese acupuncture once a week. We complete the IUIs as a means to an end. We know in-vitro fertilisation (IVF) is looming. Both my husband and I work at great corporate jobs, so money for a few hormone injections and an IUI here and there didn't break the bank, but the cost for IVF was about 10 times the price of an IUI. We sat together and planned for our IVF cycle, which we started towards the end of 2006; we hadn't even been trying a full year yet.

IVF number 1 – I respond moderately to the medication; we get a few embryos but nothing of great quality, so the doctor decides on a day 3 transfer. We get a negative. I cry a river, but soon, we are planning the next cycle, which just makes me excited and so incredibly hopeful.

Now, I know what to expect, and I ask the doctors to increase the hormone injections a little, so I can produce more viable eggs. They never want to give more medicine than necessary with PCOS as the doctors always worry about your ovaries producing more eggs than is safe for you, which can be a painful experience of extreme bloating, sharp shooting pains in your back and shoulders, and extreme fatigue. However, they agreed to up my dose.

IVF number 2 – my response is better than average. I produce a few more eggs than IVF1, the sperm looks good, and they use intracytoplasmic sperm injection (ICSI) with endometrial scratching (sounds freakish) this time to forcibly inject the sperm into the eggs. If that alone doesn't make you feel like half a couple, then I don't know what does. They have to force your husband's sperm into your egg to achieve the baby that you have both been longing for? It defeats you. "Am I meant to be a mom?" "Why do I have to force this process?"

I get to test day and haven't started bleeding – YAY! I take a pregnancy test before I go for my blood test, and it is positive!!!! Those two lines are a magic sight to behold, I still have that test. I can hardly believe it; WE FINALLY MADE IT! I'm shocked, and so is my husband. We celebrate and wave our hands in the air like we just don't care.

My beta bloods are doubling beautifully, and we wait for the 6-week scan – there is a heartbeat! We go away on holiday and tell all our family and friends that we have finally done it and achieved what we so badly wanted! I don't feel very pregnant, but then again, I don't know what it's like to be pregnant. I take my first sonar to show our family, and my mother-in-law laminates the scan, which turns it black. My heart sinks; my only photo of my baby has turned black.

We go for the 8-week scan, and we wait for that beautiful sound of a beating heart. There isn't one. I've Googled (again) what an 8-week-old fetus looks like, and when I see the scan, I know. This isn't what it should look like. I know that this isn't to be before the doctor even says anything. I went for the dilation and curettage (D&C) to remove the tissue of my baby from my uterus that same day. The baby is tested and comes back with an extremely rare chromosomal defect called Warkany Syndrome 2, trisomy 8 and female. This leads me into a very dark hole of depression and questioning myself. I grieve hard. I don't like to think of those days after my D&C; in fact, I don't remember much except for a deep aching in my heart.

By this stage, I'm feeling like a veteran and joined an online community of TTC ladies who I am still friends with today. We chat all day, I do very little of what I'm supposed to be doing, and I'm always researching new ways to treat PCOS and poor-quality sperm.

> *TIP: Don't let TTC consume every second of your day. It reduces you to a former version of you. No amount of research will change the current situation.*

With the IVF blinkers, you have one goal, and you do whatever it takes to achieve that goal. You inject your stomach through the bruises. Your whole day or even week is made when you find follicles on your scan that could turn out to be your baby! And when it doesn't, the world crashes HARD, it takes a few months to recover, and then, you are back on the IVF horse with hope coursing through your blood again. Rinse and repeat. Each time, your soul breaks a little.

We went through IVF number 3 and 4, changing medication and transfer days. Nothing. Now the doctors are talking about donor sperm and donor eggs.

INFERTILITY SUCCESS

> *TIP: This topic comes up way too soon for almost all couples. When doctors don't know the answer to the failures, they are very quick to blame the egg and sperm quality. Don't be bullied into this route too soon.*

My husband tells me that he thinks he can handle the thought of donor eggs but not donor sperm. With those IVF blinkers on, we decided to try donor eggs. We are sent emails of profiles; in South Africa, eggs are donated anonymously. The only thing I have to go on is a single grainy photo of our donor in primary school. She looks a bit like me, and so we start again. She donates, and there are a whopping two eggs, far fewer than I ever produced. They fertilize and are transferred. I'm so incredibly hopeful as "its quality and not quantity!" It doesn't work.

Next, I do a shared cycle with someone I had met online in my TTC community. She has no egg issues, her husband's sperm is a huge issue, and they need to use donor sperm, so to reduce the cost of her cycle, she offers me half her eggs. The doctors agree, and we are off again. This time, it is even worse as she produces only one egg for me, and the doctors tell me they won't transfer. At this stage of the game, the doctors know me and won't put the stress on me to attempt the two week wait. Quite amusing when you have spent most of your life savings at a clinic with absolutely no outcome. We are on failed IVF number 6.

My husband, bless him, has endured test after test. I have had every blood test known to mankind. The clinic wants to do expensive DNA testing on us. They have nothing but more questions to answer my incessant questioning. This is the end; my husband tells me. I acknowledge this. I'm exhausted from almost four years of infertility, hormone therapy, and utter sadness. "We cannot continue to bash our heads against a brick wall and expect the outcome to be different," he says. I have nothing left in me. It takes me a few months before I decide that we should look into adoption. My husband is on board and excited to be looking in a new direction.

We find a social worker in our area, and she requests a meeting with us. It's a strange meeting. Why do we want a child? What type of child would we like? Nobody else has these types of meetings before they fall pregnant, but here we are, being interrogated by someone as to why SHE thinks we would be good parents. We leave the meeting feeling quite defeated. There are courses we need to attend and loopholes in the law that make me feel very uncomfortable.

Meanwhile, all my friends are getting married and getting pregnant, one after the other. I distance myself from them. I find it increasingly difficult to be happy for them when I'm dying on the inside. It seems such a natural thing that everyone around me can just fall pregnant at the drop of a hat. My hat is still mid-air at this point.

In late 2009, after six failed IVFs and a bucket of tears, I noticed a post on social media from the company that we got our egg donor from. They are advertising "a fertility astrologer, Nicky Smuts-Allsop." I even laugh out loud. How *in the* actual world, can the moon and the stars predict when we are going to fall pregnant? I decide "well, what do I have to lose here?" I sent her a message and got a reply. She can see us the following week, and we both need to send her our exact time, date, and place of birth. Her costs are average, far, far less than an IVF, and about the same as a specialist appointment. I must say I am reluctant; what if she says a baby is not in our future? Will I accept that answer?

We Skype with Nicky, a very confident woman who knows her way around a natal chart. She sends us our charts and the best times to conceive in the next year. My husband's chart tells her that his luckiest time would be April 2010. She actually calls it a "once in a lifetime" lucky chance and would bet money on it being successful; she seems genuinely excited to tell us this news. She highly recommends that we do an embryo transfer (with our own genetic material!) in late April/May 2010 for the best chance of success.

This also happens to be the date my sister has set for her wedding, and I am the maid of honor. I started with the injections to suppress my hormones whilst at her wedding. That night, I am rolling drunk, and my husband has to carry me on his shoulder to our hotel room. I am singing to the world in my drunken state, and he has to inject me with hormones. I think to myself, "well, if this is how it starts, can you imagine how it will end?" Little do I know.

We start IVF number 7 at a *new* fertility clinic with a doctor that I can relate to, does not question me, and is keen to try line up the embryo transfer to be around the time I requested. I respond very well – as in 20+ eggs well. I've never responded like this to any of the previous IVF cycles. Out of all the eggs retrieved, we end up with 17 viable embryos! My husband turned 31 on the 4th of May, and two days later, on the 6th of May, (which also happened to be the same date of my D&C two years earlier) we transferred four viable embryos. This was it; it was going to happen now or never. I had absolutely nothing left in my tank for any further IVFs, and our application for adoption was already in motion. I asked for the maximum amount that the clinic was willing to transfer, and four embryos it was.

It's test day. I haven't started bleeding yet, which is the first good sign. I'm too scared to test at home. We go for the beta blood test, and the phone call that changes our lives happens just after noon on test day. "You are pregnant.," the most magical words you can ever hear in your life. My beta blood test was quite high at the time, so I was hoping it might be twins. Two days later, it had more than doubled.

We arrive at the fertility clinic for our 6-week scan. At the back of our minds, we are saying to ourselves, "This cannot possibly be happening." Stressful minutes pass by until the doctor arrives. I can't even look at my husband for fear of just crying. "I can't let him down at this point," I think. It can't happen again to us; please, God, no.

The doctor scans me and says, "It looks like all four have implanted; you are pregnant with quadruplets."

MIC * DROP.

I've never been more shocked in my life. I couldn't speak or even think straight. The next two weeks go by in a blur of excitement and fear. FOUR babies.

> *TIP: I caution readers here not to transfer as many embryos as I did. We were in a desperate place and I knew this was the end of the road for fertility treatment. My clinic did advise me against transferring more than 2 embryos, which I chose to ignore due to my poor history with IVF. A higher order multiple pregnancy should not be the end goal as it is a very high-risk pregnancy, both for the babies and for mom.*

The 8-week scan arrives, and as pre-warned, one baby has not made it. We are now pregnant with very alive triplets!! The unbelievable joy of seeing three individual sacks, each containing a baby WITH a heartbeat that *you made with your own DNA* is incredible. I can't ever describe that feeling to anyone.

We went from infertile to pregnant with triplets all with the help of a fertility astrologer. I have never in my wildest dreams ever thought that I would fall pregnant using the advice of an astrologer. I've been asked this many times and have spoken to Nicky about the "placebo" effect – did we fall pregnant because I believed or because it was just simply our time? To be honest, it doesn't really matter, but Nicky was incredibly accurate with everything that she shared with us.

Our triplet girls arrived at 33 weeks at Sandton Medi-clinic, Johannesburg, South Africa, on the 6th of December. It was a difficult pregnancy. I was terrified that they would not live or make it through the birth. I used to watch them move in my belly constantly, yet the self-doubt was always present. I was admitted to hospital at 32 weeks on strict bed rest, and they arrived one week later due to pre-eclampsia.

It was a very special, yet stressful birth. I had three pediatricians on call. As my doctor was cutting me open, he reminded me of how far I had come. I had to pinch myself. My first daughter, baby A was born at 08:22; she was quiet, cried a little, and was whisked to the NICU at 2.0 kg. Next, baby C was born at 08:23 with a loud cry at 1.8 kg, and then, last was baby B, born in the same minute as her sister, at 08:23, weighing in at 1.7kg with a cry and a big pee on me. None required oxygen or ventilation and all three remained in NICU for five weeks whilst they learnt to drink milk and regulate their temperatures.

The first few months of my children's lives were very stressful. I don't remember too much. It was feed, diaper change, sleep, repeat for many months; being 7 weeks premature makes one feel you are in the newborn stage for a very long time. All of a sudden, we were celebrating their first birthday, and I don't remember a thing about the first year.

We consulted with Nicky on a career opportunity when the girls were 5 months old. Nicky gave us great advice but also warned of another lucky fertile time coming up for me. We joked that we were done with our family and that we were not interested in pursuing IVF ever again. Fast forward a few months later, and I'm feeling unwell. I am nauseated and exhausted, working full time in a corporate career, and also raising triplet toddlers. I haven't had much of a cycle since the girls were born; first, I was expressing breastmilk, and then I was just trying to survive.

I'm on day 120-something. One morning, I wake up and immediately need to vomit; I feel my breasts, and they are so painful. As a complete and utter joke, I dig up an old pregnancy test that has surely expired. I pee on it and turn it over to continue changing diapers and feeding babies. There are two lines on the test, and immediately, I think I've used an ovulation test strip, but I check again, and it says HCG – a mother fucking pregnancy test. I'm pregnant. ***Naturally.*** Without a million injections, scans, embryo transfers, or money spent.

Doctors told me I'd never be able to have children. ***Angrily, I laugh out loud until I puke.*** "It's because you were relaxed," people say. How on earth am I relaxed with toddler triplets? Our son joined our family when the girls were 2 years old – four children under 3 years old. I was in survival mode.

My girls have just turned 11 years old, and my son is 9 years old. There are days I don't cope. I go to bed with my eyes crossed from pure exhaustion. Then, I wake up at 3 a.m. and lie in bed planning the next day to the minute. Some days, I laugh at the situation I find myself in. I wanted to have children so badly that God pulled a massive prank; he heard all the prayers simultaneously and sent them one after the other.

I'm grateful beyond words, I love my children with every single fiber of my being and will protect them for as long as there is breath in my body, but let me tell you something, it's not easy. It's the most difficult thing I've ever had to do to raise four children to be respectful, kind, loving, humble, and thankful. I think we have done a pretty awesome job thus far.

INFERTILITY SUCCESS

Unlock a special video message from Raylene and receive a free gift when you scan this code!

Raylene is mom to 4 beautiful children - triplet girls and a son. The road to becoming parents was not an easy one for Raylene and her husband, the part about leaving contraceptives and get pregnant the next month was a fairytale not to be seen in this lifetime for Raylene. After, what felt like a lifetime of doctor visits, tests, injections and pure determination did Raylene finally birth her own very alive triplets. The story is not the traditional one but if it helps just one other person reading this book then it was all worth it.

> "Everything will be okay in the end. If it's not okay, it's not the end" ~ John Lennon

SECONDARY INFERTILITY: OUR JOURNEY OF HOPE

Ilonka Markram

White-hot blinding rage ….

That is all I felt as I stormed out of the gynecologist's office to my car. "You are too fat to fall pregnant;" his words bounced around in my head. Not overweight, not unhealthy, too FAT! "Go home and lose as much weight as you can in the next four months. Then, come back for hormone treatment, so we can get you pregnant …"

I did not go to the gynecologist's office to have a baby. I was there to find out why I was in so much pain every month. When my period came, even my thigh muscles ached and contracted with the cramping. My mom has endometriosis and my sister, PCOS. I wanted to find out if I had these conditions and what was causing my pain. I was just so tired of the pain …

The only way to diagnose why I was having so much pain was a laparoscopic procedure.

> *TIP: Some period pain is normal but severe period pain or a change in period patterns may be indicative of an underlying problem. The only way to diagnose endometriosis or fibroids is a laparoscopy.*

My laparoscopy revealed everything was normal except for one ovary having grown onto a scar from a previous surgery. Per the gynecologist, this meant this ovary was sterile. He assured me the remaining ovary would produce an egg every month and not affect fertility, and then, he gave me the *"fat speech."* Well, that would be the LAST time he saw me!

My husband and I had been married for four years and were always careful when intimate. We talked about starting a family the next year. I was studying for my honours degree and wanted to finish it before starting our family.

In April, I took a few days off to study but was incredibly tired. I was falling asleep behind my books. I noticed being nauseous after taking my supplements in the morning. I thought I was probably crazy but asked my husband to buy a pregnancy test on the way home.

The next morning, I took the test. Even as the fluid moved over the window on the test, there was a plus sign. I was pregnant! Ironically, it was about four months after my gynecologist visit.

I was in shock! I was still studying. We had a long daily commute to work. This was NOT our plan. Our plan was to start our family *next year*! I did not feel ready for all of this. My pregnancy was confirmed via blood test the next day; I was about a month along.

Soon, the nausea was unbearable. The medicine given by my gynecologist did not help much. I was looking forward to week 12 when I was told the vomiting would stop.

But it didn't.

I vomited every day until I was six months along and lost 22 pounds during this time. I couldn't stand the smell of pretty much anything. I was constantly hungry and struggled to keep food down.

Around week 12, I also developed sciatica, lower back pain radiating through my hips and making it hard to walk. Every time I stood up, I had to stand a while and wait for the pain to subside before I could move. This did not abate until after my baby was born.

I was nauseous, constantly hungry, and in pain. I didn't really feel a connection to my baby and often felt as if an alien was growing inside me. I was so confused, knowing I should be enjoying my pregnancy but struggling to stay connected.

We finally managed to move closer to work when I was 36 weeks pregnant. It was a huge relief that we did not need to drive an hour to work and back every day.

After a hard pregnancy, our baby was born at 39 weeks via C-section. I had a terrible reaction, known as "the shakes," to the spinal block. It started shortly after my spinal block and lasted hours into recovery. The lady with whom I was sharing a room said it looked like I was having an epileptic seizure.

I struggled to breastfeed, and the nurses were no help, even telling me I had no milk.

> *TIP: There are a lot of myths around breastfeeding – don't believe them. If you are struggling, consult a nurse practitioner or contact La Leche League. Many mothers have come to know that maternity nurses are NOT lactation consultants.*

Eventually, we got it right. But it took hours and hours. I was still waiting to feel the bond I was told would be there.

Then, it was time to go home. I was scared out of my mind! How was I going to care for this little baby at home?

Eventually, we settled into a rhythm. I had quite a few varicose veins and ended up needing daily injections the first week to prevent blood clots. There was a lot of bleeding. Having been told bleeding postpartum is normal, I thought nothing of it.

After two weeks, I started feeling ill. I had no appetite, horrible nightmares about dropping my baby, nausea, dizziness, and sleeplessness. Finally, I went to the doctor and was diagnosed with anemia and prescribed an iron supplement.

For the first three weeks, babies are quiet. They eat, sleep, and poop. After three weeks, they become more animated. I noticed he was crying more than usual. It steadily increased until he was crying 12 hours a day. From 6:00 in the morning until 6:00 in the afternoon. It was terrible. I had horrible thoughts. Sometimes, I had to leave him in his crib and walk in the garden to calm down.

Eventually, I phoned the clinic sister, who advised me to see his pediatrician. He was diagnosed with colic. We got some medicine and tips on how to cope and were told it would resolve itself. I pushed through a few more days, but it was too much. I phoned the clinic nurse again; I was losing my mind. She recommended taking him to a chiropractor. We made an appointment and could see an improvement after only one session. Four sessions in total, and the colic was at a manageable level! It eventually resolved when he was four months old. Finally, I felt the bond with my baby I was waiting for.

Looking back, I believe I had undiagnosed postpartum depression. I never spoke up at my doctor visits.

> *Tip: If you feel sad and hopeless all the time after having your baby, please speak to your doctor; it's not shameful, and there is nothing wrong with you. Look after yourself so you can look after your baby!*

One of my biggest problems was that I had no tribe. We had just moved to a new city and had not made friends yet. I had no one to turn to for advice, no one to give me a break when I was overwhelmed. My husband was supportive, but he was not there during the day when I was slowly losing my mind. Our parents were far away, and we were the first of our friends to have a baby.

> *TIP: It's so important to find a tribe. Join a mom and babe class. Check out the classes at your local baby clinic. You may make a friend or two!*

For a good while, we felt that one baby was enough to complete our family. It had been a hard process, and we could just not go through it all again. We loved our little boy and enjoyed him very much, but we became concerned that he would be lonely growing up alone.

When he was about two years old, we started talking about a sibling for our son. We had felt it would be better for him to grow up with a brother or sister. Both of us had siblings and could not imagine growing up alone. By this stage, enough time had passed for me to heal from my first pregnancy and birth, at least to a degree that I felt ready to try again.

After a few months of trying, I went for a medical check-up for insurance purposes, and my doctor saw that my thyroid was very swollen. I had been extremely tired, to the point of falling on stairs because I could not lift my feet high enough. My hair had been falling out, and I had terrible insomnia. All of these I had attributed to high stress levels due to work. Blood tests, sonars, and a specialized X-ray revealed that only half of my thyroid was functional. I was put onto Eltroxin to replace the lost hormone. It took four months before I started feeling better, and I had to have blood tests every six weeks to reach my optimum medication level.

> *TIP: I would encourage all women to have their thyroid levels checked out occasionally. It is important to have an extended thyroid panel done as they show different issues. The symptoms are so easy to shrug off due to stress, hormone imbalances, or depression.*

During this time, my depression came back with a vengeance, a lovely side effect of the underactive thyroid called "chemical depression." I was suicidal at some stages, crying all the way to work every morning and having thoughts of self-harm on the way home in the afternoon. This time, I spoke up, and my doctor prescribed an antidepressant and a sleeping tablet. He also advised that we put our pregnancy dream on the back burner for a year as I needed to be on the antidepressant for that long.

After the year had lapsed, I went off the medication with my doctor's guidance. I was scared to let go of what I saw as a crutch, but I was determined to make it work! I decided to embark on a journey to become healthier while we worked on our baby dream. I wanted my body to be healthy for my baby, with no chemicals due to medication.

Being at a healthier weight would also increase fertility. I joined a ladies gym and worked out up to four days a week. I also joined a weight loss program at the same time. I was losing weight and feeling good!

I consulted with my GP, and he referred me to a gynecologist. I instantly disliked him. He did not ask my name or take down my medical history. I really did not feel like he had my best interests at heart and asked to be referred to another gynecologist.

Tip: It is very important to have a good relationship with your gynecologist. You need to be able to be open and honest with them. You need to be able to ask questions. Remember, this doctor will be a part of your journey from beginning to end.

This time, I ended up at a female gynecologist. Wow, what an eye opener to be able to speak to someone who has actually experienced pregnancy and childbirth! It was priceless! She looked over the results of my blood test (the same tests used by the previous gynecologist). She said I should wait three months to fall pregnant as my tests showed elevated blood sugar levels, and I would run the risk of gestational diabetes if we did not get it under control first. I would also need to take the medication for the duration of my pregnancy to keep my blood sugar levels stable. I was very disappointed at extending our pregnancy plan again, but I felt that she was helping me be healthier on my journey and increasing chances of falling pregnant by waiting a bit longer.

I discussed my previous pregnancy with her openly and honestly. I told her everything that had happened and how I had felt. We spoke about my C-section and how horrible it had been for me. I also spoke about our journey of trying to fall pregnant and how it had not happened yet. I could not understand how easily it had happened the first time and how long we had been trying unsuccessfully now.

She said it was called secondary infertility.

We needed to wait three months and then try to fall pregnant for six months. If still unsuccessful, she wanted to do a laparoscopy to make sure there were no issues on the inside.

> *TIP: Your doctor will provide you with advice and a way forward. While it's important to follow their advice, if you feel the need to have tests done earlier, speak up; it is your journey, and they are on it with you, but it is still YOUR journey.*

We followed her instructions carefully. I tracked my cycles, and we timed our intimacy around it. Every month, I managed to convince myself that this was the month it would finally happen because I was tired or felt some cramping or my boobs were sore. I always waited until I was a day late before testing.

Every time it came back negative, I died a little inside. I wondered if I had done something wrong. Maybe because I felt so negative during my first pregnancy or because I struggled to connect with my baby? Maybe I did not deserve to become a mother again?

During the time we tried for baby number two, I attended a few baby showers, always having to field questions about when the next baby would come. Or if I chose to talk, I would hear that "at least we already had one." The fact that we already had one child did not make the ache in our hearts any less.

> *TIP: Never downplay another person's pain; we all experience it differently, especially if that person has not made peace with their pain. I wish I had been strong enough to say this to people I shared my dream with instead of crying on the inside.*

Then, the six months were complete and still no pregnancy. The laparoscopy would have a large co-payment, and we just did not have the funds for it. We talked about it and decided to resign ourselves to only having one child. Our hearts just could not deal with the pain of failure every time my cycle came. Having a baby naturally was the only option for us; we did not have funds for further treatments or IVF.

A couple of weeks later, we went to a restaurant for our wedding anniversary. I felt a bit adventurous and decided to order dishes I had not tried before. The food was delicious. The next morning, when I woke up, I thought about the dishes I had eaten, – dishes I would not normally **ever** think about eating, including blue cheese. Was this a pregnancy craving? There was one pregnancy test left. I decided to take it; I might as well, right?

It was positive! I danced around the bathroom and shouted for my husband. I could not believe it! Finally, after we had given up, it happened!

I went for a blood test, so we could be sure. They told me to phone at 8:00 that evening for the results. I phoned and got my positive results to the tune of Katy Perry's *Fireworks*, and that song will forever hold a special place in my heart.

After a few weeks, we went for our first sonar and saw our little dot. I was about five weeks pregnant, and already, the nausea was unpleasant. I had already started vomiting daily. The gynecologist gave me a script to help the symptoms but advised that it might be due to my underactive thyroid. We would need to monitor my thyroid levels carefully throughout my pregnancy. The sciatica pain also returned around the 12-week mark, and I was still vomiting daily, sometimes multiple times. This time around, it continued until I delivered my baby.

At our 20-week scan, the gynae expressed concern that he was smaller than anticipated and sent us for a specialized scan. I was stressed out of my mind. I had read that thyroid issues could cause birth defects if not properly controlled during the pregnancy. We went for the scan at 22 weeks. The scan is so detailed that you can see the blood pumping through the little heart and kidneys. It was quite amazing, and we learned we were expecting another boy. The scan showed that there was nothing wrong with our baby; he was perfect. What a relief! Finally, at 38 weeks, he was delivered via C-section. My doctor made certain to use different medicine in my spinal block to minimize the shakes. I still experienced the side effect but nowhere near as badly as the previous time. When I heard his little cry, I just wanted to hold him.

Back in the room, after recovery, he was brought in to breastfeed. The nurse helped him to latch while I was still shaking. He was a superstar and managed to feed straight away. I held him and kept on thinking how amazing it was that he grew inside me and I was holding him in my arms. I finally got to feel that magical feeling of being in love with my baby. There is really nothing to compare it to. I also felt a bit sad knowing that I had not experienced it instantly with my first baby.

We went home and fell into routine again. About a week later, I was sitting on the couch with the sun falling over my shoulder, and I noticed the whites of his eyes were yellow. Yellow eyes are a sign of jaundice. We took him to the ER immediately. He had a blood prick test, and the results were not worrying. We were advised to put him in the sun twice a day and feed him every three hours, even through the night. I had to wake him to feed if he was sleeping since the milk flushed his system. I set alarms on my phone and fed him every three hours until he was six weeks old. It was exhausting!

At his 6-week check-up, he was cleared, and we could now go to on-demand feeding. I spoke to the pediatrician about him pulling faces; he would make a face as if he was tasting something really bad and often had a sour milk smell. He was diagnosed with silent reflux. This meant smaller feeds, sleeping at an angle, and medicine to make the milk thicker. I worried about him vomiting and choking in his sleep. This increased my anxiety; I kept checking on him when he was sleeping, too scared to leave him on his own.

At my 6-week check-up, I spoke to my gynecologist about how I was feeling. It was hard, but I realized I needed to feel better. I loved my baby, but I was always sad. I felt alone and unworthy, and I was crying a lot. This time, I was diagnosed with postnatal depression and put onto medication. She advised me to speak to my doctor when I wanted to stop breastfeeding to see if I needed to go back onto my anti-depressant again.

> *TIP: If you are afraid to leave your baby for fear they're going to die, are crying most of the day, or have overwhelming feelings of isolation, please speak to your doctor. These could be indicators of postpartum depression.*

Our boys have an almost 5-year gap. Although we wanted a smaller gap, I think with the challenges both babies had, along with my depression, we would not have coped if they had been born closer together.

When our youngest son was six years old, we discovered that he is autistic, with ADHD and SPD. And so, we embarked on our next adventure. This journey would teach us about the importance of family bonds and finding and leaning on your tribe.

We love both our boys immensely and celebrate the differences between them. Each one is unique and perfect in his own way.

Sometimes, a baby makes us wait a bit, and although it is hard, don't give up. What I have learned through this journey is that things don't necessarily happen when we expect or want them to but when they are supposed to. Lean on your people when you need to, and find the doctor that is right for you. Ask for help, educate yourself, and never be afraid to speak up.

MORE STORIES OF HELP AND HOPE FOR YOUR JOURNEY

Unlock a special video message from Ilonka and
receive a free gift when you scan this code!

Ilonka Markram is a wife and mom to two boys. They live in Johannesburg, South Africa, with their pack of dachshunds. She works full time as an accountant and spends her spare time with her family. She is invested in her kids and takes a role in their extramural activities. She believes in raising her family based on gentle parenting principles. Her youngest son is neuro-divergent, and she is a strong advocate for inclusion of these special humans. She hopes that her chapter will give hope to anyone on a similar path to becoming a mom.

PREPARING ELLIANA'S WOMB

Harmony Bacon

My husband woke up startled, slapping the bed and saying, "Where is she? Honey, wake up; where is she?"

I responded "SHE WHO!? What SHE are you talking about?!"

He sat up and looked around and said, "Our baby girl."

I pointed to my large belly saying, "I'm pretty sure it's a boy, but #2 is still cooking; it was a dream." I asked him to describe her, and it was precious how he shared every detail. This confirmed a dream I had of a little girl before I even got pregnant with our first child. It's incredible how God gave both of us a glimpse of the little girl we were meant to seek out and adopt.

When our second son was six months old, all of a sudden, while singing at church, my husband pulled me down while holding our sleeping boy and said, "WE HAVE TO PRAY!"

I sat and bowed my head with him as he rattled off the most intense detailed prayer about our daughter's mother. I was very confused but agreed and prayed with him for protection and her health. After this, I dove into adoption stuff, assuming it was time to start the search. I paddled out into the pool of adoption twice without my husband fully on board. I got nowhere; every door shut over and over. Despair filled my soul. We even applied for foster care and got turned down because we were too honest! Talk about disappointment!

With a heavy heart and lots of tears, I asked God to take away my desire to adopt. I wanted to have joy with the two boys God blessed us with and not have my heart discontent with wanting more. I wanted to live with joy again, seeing the world through my boys' eyes and for that to be enough. As I prayed, I asked God for a sign. I asked God to say through my husband the words, 'It's time to adopt." As I lifted my head to say "Amen," the air smelled sweeter and my heart lighter.

I found my joy and loved every moment with my boys; there was no more wanting. I praised God each year for this time with them. After my 37th birthday, my health started declining. By summer, I was feeling poorly in general. I was seeing floaters in my eyes, experiencing abdominal, kidney, bladder pain, painful sex, weird periods, and hypoglycemia. Thirty-seven wasn't looking so hot for me!

My husband and I continued to lay foundations for our businesses and bought our house. My massage clients had been asking me to teach them more about essential oil uses. I started looking into how to teach them and seeking a God-fearing community to help with teaching materials.

Mid-summer, my husband was telling me about his business plans, then casually said, "Once this business loan is paid off, it is time to adopt." My mouth just hung open, shocked that the words that I prayed for came out of his mouth! I knew God was behind those five words.

It was shortly after this amazing statement that I found a local essential oil group. During the first meeting of this group, we were asked to write our WHY (why do you want to build a business). My "why" was to pay for the kids' tuition and the adoption.

I started attending the community meet ups, and during one of the meetings, someone brought a biofeedback scanner called a Zyto Scan. I had no idea what it was exactly, but I was intrigued to say the least. I was excited to have the scan, hoping to get some insight into why I wasn't feeling very good. The results showed that my hormones were all over the place and recommended Progessence Plus, Endoflex, Frankincense, Femigen, and PD 80/20 to bring my body back to homeostasis. I had not used any of those oils or vitamins from my company. I added them to my next order.

I made a doctors' appointment a week later, and she said my iron was low and that I had poor cellular health and suggested we start there. Ha! That's what my company's supplements were all about, so I ordered their mulit-vitamin called Master Formula and enzymes called Essentialzyme to start with.

My doctor sent me to get a contrast MRI of my pelvis as this would give us the most answers. The MRI results of my pelvis were unremarkable, so she then referred me to an OBGYN.

When the OBGYN examined me, she felt what I felt and called to get the MRI re-read. The results came back quickly with three fibroids – 7 cm, 5 cm, and 2 cm. My order of vitamins arrived, and I had my doubts about the possibility of changing my diagnosis, but I was willing to try. I spoke healing over my body, my hormones, my health, and my uterus as I put frankincense over my uterus every time I used the restroom.

A follow-up ultrasound was scheduled for a few months later to see if my fibroids had grown. I knew I had until then to see what

God and his amazing craftsmanship could accomplish along with these vitamins and essential oils. I was feeling remarkable within two weeks of introducing everything, and all my symptoms had improved! I couldn't wait for January to come. Even the painful sex had started to get better. I knew the fibroids were gone and couldn't wait to tell the world about what had happened to me.

The morning of the ultrasound appointment, I had the community meet up, and they prayed for me. As the technician performed the ultrasound, I told her how excited I was to find out if they had gone away. She was very quiet and very busy pushing that thing ALL over up in there. As she finished, she said, "I can't find them." She was very concerned that I had been misdiagnosed or that there was something wrong with the notes or her machine. I reassured her that it was the frankincense essential oil that did it, explaining that it's high in monoterpenes, which can make unhealthy cells healthy.

She said, "Like what the wise men brought Jesus?"

I said, "YES! If it's good enough for the Savior of the world, it's good enough for me!

It was an incredible time in our lives! God was preparing me for something amazing. I felt His hand holding mine as we walked by faith in my health, our businesses, and the adoption process! We had gone to our local adoption agency and a few adoption lawyers. All said, our search for our little Spanish girl would be a long wait. The lawyer suggested we get a home study done in case one of his friends in Texas received word from the border. The home study was scheduled for March! I was so excited and nervous. I went over our house with a fine-tooth comb to make sure she wouldn't find anything that could prevent it from going through. Alan's business loans were almost paid off, and my office was busier than ever.

A past doula client asked me to consider being a surrogate for her. I was excited, it was something my husband and I were willing to do. I declined because it gave me the idea about embryo adoption to complete our own family. I was reminded about a video of a missionary in Africa who wanted to experience pregnancy and birth. She was going to give life to someone's unused embryos from IVF. I had Alan watch it on YouTube. The National Embryo Donation Center has thousands of babies waiting. He was intrigued to say the least.

I said, "What if we surrogate for ourselves? We could pick race and possibly even the sex." We went for a family walk, and we all made a pros and cons list and a questions list. By the end of the evening, we all had agreed that I had to do further research. I started calling all the embryo donation and snowflake adoption centers. Snowflake is a sweet term for a frozen embryo, no two are the same, each is beautifully created.

I called each center and asked if I was able to pick the baby's ethnicity and gender. Provided that answer was yes, I asked if they shipped the baby and I would have an IVF doctor here take over care and insertion. Or would I need to go to the location, and if so, how many visits? What medical history did they have on the parents? Are adoptions considered open or closed? And what was the cost? Most open adoptions went up in price due to lawyer fees to draw up agreements for both sides. Cost also rose if the baby was shipped, and I would need a local IVF doctor. Some also had age and marriage requirements. Through these questions, my search narrowed to just a few centers.

Based on these questions, we were able to narrow down the 20 centers to one – the NEDC. The National Embryo Donation Center was the place we felt God led us to.

NEDC required just three visits. One was to check my anatomy and meet the doctor, embryo nurse, and our assigned adoption specialist. The second was to make sure the medications did what they should do along with a trial run implantation, and the third visit was implantation.

From that point on, the doors flew open; it was amazing how fast the process was moving. I had a serious learning curve to learn the lingo and process and medications. With the fibroids gone, I wanted to make sure I did everything possible to make sure our embryo had the perfect home to grow in. I got busy researching how to further improve my health for implantation. While teaching about replacing household chemicals for clean organic products, I found that MANY chemicals were endocrine disruptors. Most cause fetal development problems or miscarriages. Many products contained fake estrogen that blocks hormone receptor sites, which would wreak havoc on my hormones.

I wanted to protect this little girl before she was even placed in my womb, so I continued each month switching out a room in our house with chemical-free products from my company. I even switched my makeup. I was so incredibly grateful to have found a company that had all the products I needed to keep my uterus safe for my soon-to-be adoption. This was a company with which I felt confident I could align myself and my massage business with their high standards and integrity. I knew that to give my little girl her best chance, I needed to get rid of the chemicals that came in contact with my skin, right down to the chlorine I put in the pool.

Next, I started eating only two food groups at a time, keeping fruit as a snack alone to help restore any leaks in my gut. This, in turn, allowed more nutrition to be absorbed into my cells, creating health and wellness. I cut out caffeine, soda and alcohol.

As I was teaching, I found an amazing resource for internal cleansing called "Inner Transformation Using Essential Oils'.' I found out that my uterus sits on my colon, and the stinky trash from my colon can seep into my uterus, causing it to be toxic for a developing embryo. I started the colon cleanse protocol and was impressed at how gentle it was. I was grateful it didn't make me run to the bathroom in the middle of a massage! I learned how important it was to make sure you are having a bowel movement after every meal.

A colon cleanse can help so many things. Chemicals get trapped in our intestines, causing all sorts of havoc in our body like gas, headaches, hormone imbalances, depression, anxiety, insomnia, poor memory, allergies, body odor, and frequent colds. My health improved by leaps and bounds. My next Zyto scans came back better and better. I had lost 20 pounds and was feeling AMAZING!

We applied to the NEDC, got approved in September, and were given our initial appointment to meet and be examined by Dr. G. on December 13th. We booked our flight to Tennessee. The IVF nurse started emailing, explaining all the medication and steps that would have to happen before and after to prep the body. This was terrifying for me. I had never taken hormones and did not want to start. I was so proud of my health. With my hormones and health finally improving, it was hard to consider putting drugs in my body that could possibly change everything.

I asked my husband to pray over me and rebuke my fears and pride. I heard the word SURRENDER as if God himself spoke to me. I crumbled and agreed to allow His will for this child to be. I would be His vessel for whatever the process held.

Friday the 13th was full of blessings! We shared our story of waiting and seeking our little Hispanic girl with the matching staff. There wasn't a dry eye in the room as we poured our hearts out, telling the story of how we had sought and prayed for seven years and to have answered prayers lead us there.

Dr. G. then met with us, and I shared about healing my fibroids, my previous health, and the restoration of it all. He shared about the risk of miscarrying as well as the procedure and that success was 50/50. He also told us that if we chose a genetically tested embryo, they would only allow one baby at a time with three chances. Dr. G. asked me to stop all the essential oils and hormone supports I was taking to make sure the hormone pills did exactly as they should, and I surrendered and agreed. Alan and I held each other's hands as God held our hearts.

The staff needed to know if we wanted an open or closed adoption. We explained that we didn't want to be in one camp or another because we just needed to find her. We both wanted a closed adoption because that keeps the cost down with lawyers, but we were willing to work with an open one if needed. The matching staff came with one file from an open adoption that matched what we were looking for.

> *TIP: Centers want to get all their embryos adopted. The more open you are, the faster you will find your baby. They listen, and you tell them what you are hoping for. Some centers don't allow you to choose, and some do. At NEDC, you can choose genetically tested (which is how they find out the sex) and the race. With some convincing, they helped us find our daughter.*

There was only ONE baby left, a girl, and as they opened the file, our hearts jumped from our chests. We were bursting with anticipation at the thought that this might be our little girl. We said we would take this file as our first choice. They explained that because there is only one baby left with this family, we would have to choose two more embryos as backups. They booked our next appointment for December 30th.

It was a very efficient experience, a whirlwind of meet and greets, examinations, laughter, and tears. Our emotions swirled as we walked out of their office. It was all so surreal to think that our long-awaited adoption was in the works!

We went to lunch and spoke of God's mercies and blessings throughout this entire process – how He aligned the buying of our house, the expansion of my husband's business, and becoming a distributor and teacher for my company to pave the way here. We reminisced about the doors that opened and the doors that closed but, most of all, the abundance of walking in His will and waiting in faith.

After lunch, we filled the prescription for my first hormone. I was shaking with fear as I held that pill in my hand. I was about to put it in my mouth when I looked at my husband and burst into tears. He held me and reminded me of all that God had brought us through to get here and how he was already protecting my body. I've never felt such relief from darkness as in that moment. He reminded me that God has dominion over my body. I thanked God and surrendered my body to Him while downing the little pill.

Seventeen days later, we were back in Tennessee to make sure the hormones did what needed to be done. God was faithful and protected my emotions from getting out of control. I was incredibly thankful to not be on any more drugs until it was baby time.

That week, emails from "open" adoptions poured into my inbox. I was grateful they helped me narrow down the search to just 38. Each embryo came with a doctor intake form filled out by each parent of the embryos. Some had pictures of siblings, some showed how many embryos were left and if they were genetically tested. There were so many babies that needed a warm uterus!! How was I to pick who was meant to be ours?

I know my husband's heart was set on a little Hispanic girl because he is Colombian, and his sister was adopted from there. Our dreams just showed a baby darker than us. How could we say she was Hispanic? She could have been an islander, from India, or any other race darker than us. As I prayed, I decided that I would just show my husband a picture of siblings.

After a week of reading doctor intake forms, I had narrowed it down to three pictures of siblings to show my husband. I told him, "Only God knows which child is meant to be in our family. If it is not the Hispanic baby, then it might be one of these. Which of these siblings are your daughters'?"

He didn't hesitate. He pointed and said, "This one."

I said, "You don't want to take the pictures and pray over them?"

In a matter-of-fact tone, he said, "No." Little did he know, this family had several female embryos waiting for a home, and #3029 ended up being our second and third picks. After placing holds on the embryos, the families were notified and asked to start the approval process, and lawyer agreements about visitations were drawn up. The home study seemed like it dragged on until it was finally finished on January 6th. The families approved of us to raise their babies with the agreement of one picture sent each birthday that included milestones and allowing a meeting of birth parents if she wanted to after the age of 18. We prayed, "Only you, Lord, know which child is ours, and I surrender my body to Your will for this precious puzzle piece to be born."

I continued to focus on my health, doing all I knew to insure a good transfer and a healthy uterus. I stopped the colon cleanse and started stocking my body full of vitamins and minerals that would help a growing baby. I wanted to make sure my body was ready to build this sweet baby. March 2nd was approaching quickly; it was time to start the pills and shots. Again, I prayed and felt His protection over the pills and shots required to make my uterus a happy home for this little baby. The IVF nurse emailed me each week to check in and gave us our transfer date!!! Joy exploded from us; we had the date our family would become five April 29th, 2020!

We prepared the boys' hearts and minds for the possible ups and downs of 50/50 chances. After answering all their questions, my husband and boys laid hands on me and bowed their heads. Tears of joy, surrender, love, anticipation, and pride poured over my flushed cheeks as the sweetest prayer a mother could ever hear was uttered from the mouths of her children and husband. I spoke words of thanksgiving and submission and began shots morning and night and pills three times a day. I upped the amount of Omegagize I was using to keep my blood thin for easy implantation.

Two weeks before our transfer date, I got a colonic done; the anxiety was REAL! I knew it had been months since my cleanse, so I wanted to make sure no toxins could get to my uterus. Boy, oh, boy, was I grateful when that was over! Thankfully, it wasn't as bad as I had imagined. I was ready; my colon, my arms, my uterus, and our hearts were open.

I got an email at the end of March with all sorts of warnings about Covid-19 and waivers I would have to sign to continue care for the transfer. We signed everything and made arrangements to drive up to Tennessee as a family. The drive was full of gloved hands, washing hands, masked faces, and disinfecting hands with a non-toxic hand sanitizer at every stop. My husband and I could barely sleep that night. We knew that our lives would change the next morning.

Transfer day was a beautiful day! We ate breakfast at a park close to the clinic because we didn't want to be late. I was instructed to take a valium an hour before our appointment. The walk in the park became very interesting for me, to say the least. My husband was laughing at me as we stood waiting at the door.

> *TIP: For transfer day, consider what is going to make you feel relaxed and also talk to your doctor about what they provide in terms of support in this area.*

When they came out to get us, they informed us that our Hispanic baby girl didn't survive the thawing process and that our second choice was growing and graded with an A++. They took me back, had me lay down, and within 15 minutes, I was pregnant with a Thai/British girl! I walked out of the clinic to the car shaking with an adrenaline rush and said, "Okay, let's go home as a family of five."

My 8-year-old jumped out and said, "Where is your big belly?"!

I smiled and laughed with tears in my eyes as my husband and I explained that she was the size of the tip of a pen. We explained, "Now, we pray she grows her roots deep into my uterus; just like a seed planted in soil, she was planted in my uterus." The face of quizzical understanding rolled over him as he smiled big, touched my belly, and said, "I love you little sister."

My husband and I thanked God for the mercy of being able to save two babies from the freezer. Knowing our little first baby girl was already in heaven, sitting on Jesus' lap was comforting for us. Elliana was born in her time, on January 26th at 42.6 weeks. I will forever tell her amazing story and how she touches so many hearts.

Unlock a special video message from Harmony and receive a free gift when you scan this code!

I grew up in Sarasota, Florida, where I married my high school sweetheart in 2003. I continued my education with EMT, massage therapy, paramedic, then phlebotomy. I worked for the hospital doing both massage therapy and phlebotomy. In 2006, my husband and I moved to Tennessee for him to continue his education. In 2009, after five years of enjoying trying to become pregnant, God blessed us with a boy. A year and a half later, I miscounted, and God humored us with another son. In 2010, we moved back to Sarasota, and I restarted my massage therapy practice. www.byharmonybacon.com

VICIOUS CYCLES TO VIBRANT RAINBOWS: MY STORY OF NAVIGATING INFERTILITY, IVF, TRIPLETS, AND MOTHERHOOD WITH TWINS.

Cara B. Drescher

"Life takes us on all kinds of journeys. Different paths lead to different places, but rarely does the path you choose take you where you plan to go."
Cara B.

My life journey has been one with many twists and turns, including the unexpected, extremely confusing, and uncertain path of infertility. Though my infertility journey has been the most painful adventure I've had thus far, what's gotten me through is the unwavering support of my loving husband, Dave.

We went to high school together but lost touch after graduation. We reconnected 12 years later through a mutual friend and developed a friendship. We'd get together for lunch once a week or so for many months until one day, I realized that I felt something much deeper for him. I fell in love with him long before I realized it, and by our second "official" date, I knew I wanted to have children with him.

I always knew I wanted to be a mom, but I never knew what getting there would entail. Getting pregnant is supposed to be the most natural thing in the world. So much of this journey makes you question your purpose in life, especially when you are physically incapable of doing the most natural thing in the world.

I always assumed that I'd have a baby one day. It never seemed like a question; it was just a fact. One day, I'd give birth and raise my child with my spouse. No one tells you about the possibility of having difficulty getting pregnant. All you hear is *how not to* get pregnant because it's *so* easy to get pregnant. So, when you're faced with infertility, it's like a huge slap in the face. It feels like you've been lied to your whole life.

My infertility journey really began three years before it officially bore the title "infertility." I spent three years desperately wanting to be pregnant and have a child, and then another three years going through fertility treatments and having the actual diagnosis of infertility. It was six years of dreading pregnancy announcements, looking at other people's ultrasound photos, and crying myself to sleep at night. For three years before actually trying to conceive, I was ready. Mentally, emotionally, and physically, I was ready. But financially ... that was a different story. My extremely generous parents allowed us to live in their house rent-free so that Dave could finish his degree and become the teacher he had wanted to be for so many years. We lived with them for four years following our wedding. It was a huge factor in our decision to wait to start our family, and it was directly related to our finances.

> *TIP: I often think to myself, "looking back on this entire journey, would I still wait because of our financial situation?" It's extremely important to take a look at your life from all angles and take a very large step back. You have to look at a variety of factors that go into the decision to start a family, and finances is one of them. I encourage you to be mindful of your financial situation throughout this journey. Make a pros and cons list. Draw up a monthly and even yearly budget. An equally important aspect is time. Time doesn't stop. It's not that you become "too old" or "run out of time;" it's that, sometimes, life passes you by quicker than you realize.*

Pregnancy announcements during this time became extremely distressing. I'd become enraged when someone was pregnant anywhere in my line of sight. It started with Facebook announcements. Then, it was celebrity pregnancy announcements. It then progressed to in-person announcements from friends. One morning, my parents told me that my older sister was pregnant. Unsurprisingly, I did not handle it well. I had been overwhelmingly sad about not being able to even *try* to conceive, and now, my sister was pregnant when she wasn't even trying! It just felt so unfair. Not long after, my best friend announced her first pregnancy.

I finally came to terms with their pregnancies, but it all came to a head just a few weeks after their babies were born. Dave's friend and his wife announced their first pregnancy. That news was hard to take. I sat still during their very elaborate announcement with my heart racing, choking back tears. I cried the entire ride home, refusing to even speak about it. Announcement after announcement came, and my heart was constantly being shattered into pieces. Then, one conversation changed everything.

Dave's brother called and told us that he and his wife were expecting their second child. Was every single person in the world pregnant? It just wasn't fair! When was it going to be my turn? Later that night, Dave said he was ready to start trying, regardless of our financial concerns. So, we took the plunge.

The first few months were frustrating. Every month, I'd get my period, and the pain, anger, and sadness would overwhelm me. It became clear that at our ages (35 and 37) and after nine months with no success, it was time to get help. So I made an appointment with a fertility specialist. But then, one week before the fertility appointment, our world was turned upside down.

I attended a business meeting for local prenatal wellness practitioners. I immediately felt overwhelmed and alone as everyone had kids, and it was the only thing anyone wanted to talk about. I left as early as I could, not able to hold back tears anymore. I cried myself to sleep that night.

When I awoke in the morning, my eyes were so swollen that I couldn't see clearly. I wasn't wearing my glasses, and I tripped and fell down a flight of stairs, causing a dislocated shoulder, a rotator cuff tear, and whiplash. After my shoulder surgery to repair the damage, I developed severe frozen shoulder and had a second surgery. I was unable to work for 13 months. We took six months off from trying to conceive during this ordeal as I couldn't even *use* my right arm. How was I possibly going to *be* pregnant let alone *try* to get pregnant? Taking time off was absolute torture.

When we finally saw the reproductive endocrinologist, we were met with the diagnosis of unexplained infertility. It's a difficult diagnosis to accept as there's no explanation, and, therefore, no obvious treatment. She ordered all of the typical infertility tests — blood work including AMH, FSH, Estradiol, Progesterone, and LH levels, pelvic exam, and HSG (hysterosalpingogram) and then a semen analysis for my husband. All tests came back normal — no red flags. There was nothing that would suggest *why* we couldn't get pregnant. It felt like a guessing game. She recommended starting with IUI, and our first one failed, as did the five subsequent IUIs.

TIP: The thing people tell you but is very hard to wrap your mind around during this journey is that IUI success is tricky. Statistically, if it's not successful after the first three attempts, the chances of IUI success drop dramatically. Infertility has a way of creating a distorted perception of reality. That's why I recommend what I didn't do for myself. Reach out for mental health support from a coach, counselor, or therapist. Just having someone to support you in making the decision to proceed with another IUI, move on to IVF, or take a break from treatments makes all the difference. Whatever point you're at in your journey, find the person who has the experience and can help you make the right decision for ***you***.

We couldn't afford IVF as our insurance wouldn't cover it, and our financial situation was far from secure. We were left with few options to create a family, so we began researching fertility treatment grants and were surprised to find a few grants we were qualified to apply for.

We proceeded with a grant application for a local organization and were thrilled to find out about a month later that we were approved. This particular grant afforded us $5,000 to put toward IVF with the exception of medications. We'd have to pay for the medications out of pocket. We were lucky enough to be given some money towards IVF from both sets of parents, and then, we took out an additional loan to cover the rest.

We started our first IVF cycle 14 months after our first fertility specialist appointment. Going into IVF felt terrifying. It was extremely overwhelming, and it wasn't something I ever thought I was going to need to do. At the first appointment to set everything up, I had a meltdown. I couldn't speak. I couldn't think. I could hardly breathe. My mom came to the appointment with me and took all the notes because I was struggling to fit information into my brain due to the overwhelming nature of it all. The day we started injections I began feeling more comfortable and in control of it all. I knew what I needed to do, and I felt confident that I could handle it.

> *TIP: Preparing yourself for your IVF appt is* **crucial***. I connected with two people who had previously gone through IVF —; a friend and a friend of a friend. Both were helpful, but neither could give me the exact support I needed. Ultimately, what I really needed (but didn't know existed at that time) was an infertility coach. I needed someone who had not only gone through the journey of IVF, but also who knew how to walk the journey alongside me. I needed someone who could help navigate the mountain of paperwork, appointments, testing, procedures, and terminology of it all and. Someone who could support my emotional struggle as well. Partners and friends are incredible resources, but it's not their job to know the ins*

and outs of IVF, or how to support you from an objective perspective.

Our IVF cycle resulted in seven eggs retrieved, three mature, and one fertilized (using ICSI AKA intracytoplasmic sperm injection)., and it was transferred on day 3. But our little 10+ cell embryo did not implant. Getting the call that my pregnancy test was negative felt like a knife being plunged into my heart. I had been prepared for a failed transfer, but I was **not** prepared for *zero backup embryos*. The realization that we were back at square one felt like someone ripped my heart out and then laughed at me while I was dying.

At this point, we were frustrated and unsure of our next steps. I was feeling overwhelmed, desperate, and running out of time. I rushed a grant application to another organization one month after our failed IVF cycle and was rejected.

The desperation of that rejection changed me, and I was more determined than ever to get the baby I had been wishing for my whole life. I went to work and wrote a powerful essay full of passion and raw emotion. It became my job to convince them that what I was going through was tearing me apart because that's what infertility does to you.

> "As I'm getting older, my opportunity to conceive and give birth is becoming less likely, and each day that I go through this infertility nightmare, it takes a little piece of my heart with it."

This quote was part of my personal essay for the second fertility treatment grant I won.

TIP: The power of feeling and telling your story cannot be underestimated. Fertility grants are surprisingly easy to find. Google "fertility grant" or "infertility grant" or even "fertility treatment grant," and you'll get a pretty extensive list. Don't get discouraged if you see a lot of local grants that you might not qualify for; there are plenty more that are open to national applicants (in the U.S.). Some are limited to specific age groups, religious affiliations, and so on. Some may require you to go to a specific clinic, while others allow you to go to any clinic of your choosing. The last important detail to keep in mind when you're researching your grant is that most (not all) have very strict deadlines.

Every moment of every day, I'd feel the burning question in my mind, "What's wrong with me; why can't I just get pregnant?" The emotional, and sometimes physical pain of infertility was like nothing I had ever experienced. Every fertility treatment *failed*. Every attempt at making a baby on our own *failed*. Everyone around me was pregnant or carrying an infant around. I couldn't breathe most days because the anxiety filled my body to the brim, leaving nothing left inside me. I had become an empty shell of who I once was. I was now a bitter, sad, hopeless woman with nothing to look forward to.

TIP: Infertility can feel endless and hopeless. But it doesn't have to be that way! There is always hope, and there is always an end, even if it's not in sight yet. Taking a step back and making it a point to focus on your mindset can help redirect those negative thoughts and create a new path to follow. Mindset work is a step-by-step process. The

> *purpose of working on your mindset is transforming the negative, fixed outlook on life (or specific situations) into an open-minded, full of possibilities outlook.*

One day, I started implementing small changes and began living and viewing life differently. This was the start of my new mindset and new path. These small changes altered the trajectory of my infertility journey. I went from lower than low to more empowered and stronger than I had ever been. The changes I made that brought me to that empowered place were simple yet powerful. I didn't plan on any results from these changes; I just wanted to feel better. I wanted to enjoy life again and not feel like I was under infertility's thumb.

> *TIP: When you come to the decision to implement small changes, it's essential to do it little by little and choose changes that work for* **you**. *The goal is to make changes that can distract you a little bit from your journey, while also allowing you to continue to experience your journey — just in an easier way. It's not about being so distracted that you "escape" infertility. It's about making your life easier, more pleasurable, and ultimately lessening the burden of infertility.*

I realized that I was beginning to fall into a deep hole of depression. I had previously gone through a major depression that almost destroyed my life, and I never wanted to go through that again. I recognized the signs, so I found a counselor who specialized in infertility.

> *TIP: There's no right way to seek help when it comes to mental health and infertility. For me, it was knowing that I had a previous experience with depression, and I knew what the warning signs were — feeling hopeless, unusually fatigued, persistent sadness, and a deep feeling of being unworthy of life. Those emotions are consistent with depression, and I knew what it felt like. But depression doesn't always appear that way. It can sneak up on you without anything other than just not feeling like yourself. I'm a firm believer that even without a prior history of depression, anxiety or any other mental health concerns, it's important for anyone and everyone at any stage of infertility to seek out mental health support.*

I believe my decision to get mental health support had a major impact on my eventual success. I also recognized that I needed to work on my mindset. Now, I'm not saying this is the solution, and you'll miraculously conceive once you work on your mindset. I don't really believe that. What I do believe, however, is that mindset plays a huge role in *surviving* infertility. Stress doesn't cause infertility, but it is a major component of the bigger picture.

The combination of therapy and mindset work allowed me to begin the process of getting ready to move on from infertility. I was reaching my breaking point and felt that I couldn't mentally or physically continue with the stress of this journey.

I began unintentionally making more small changes in my life. I cut my hair, which was a huge change for me. I was majorly attached to my long hair. On a more spiritual note, it lifted both literal and metaphorical weight off my shoulders. I started taking better care of my body and spirit. I took walks. I talked about what I was feeling. I didn't *pretend* that everything was okay. I shared my story. I realigned my chakras. And the biggest change I made was switching to a different fertility specialist.

> *TIP: I loved my first fertility specialist. I hated saying goodbye to her. But after spinning our wheels and doing the same things over and over without success, I knew it was time to try something different. I never realized that there could be different approaches. It took me a while to get past the guilt, and long after my infertility journey ended, I went in to see her, and she felt zero resentment toward me. Her exact words to me were, "there is no resentment here! The most important thing for me is that my patients are happy and get the results they're looking for. If I can't provide that, then I'm not the right person for them, and that's okay."* **I wish I had made the decision to get a second opinion sooner.**

Moving on to the new reproductive endocrinologist (RE), I found myself in a state of calm. I knew I was still fighting my battle, and it wasn't going to disappear until I was ready to move on or had success. But it wasn't as painful as it had been. I was no longer waking up with tears in my eyes before I even opened them. I wasn't staring hopelessly out the window. I wasn't spending every second of every day questioning my life purpose. I knew in my soul for the first time that I was so much more than my ability (or inability) to conceive.

Not long after my newfound outlook on life took hold, I prepared for my ninth IUI. We were planning a second IVF cycle with our new RE but were waiting to find out if we were approved for the second fertility grant. Our new RE wanted to try an experiment with Clomid and Letrozole at the same time in the same cycle rather than the traditional approach of one or the other. So I took both and did the IUI. It failed, but it wasn't as devastating as the previous failed attempts had been. I was actually able to laugh about it. Not because it was funny, but because it was so ridiculous that even our **ninth** IUI had failed. As a last-ditch effort, in preparation for what was to be our tenth and last IUI, my RE had me take Clomid and Letrozole again but changed the timing of each dose.

> *TIP: What made this particular doctor stand out was that after that first IUI with her that wasn't successful, she tried something different. It was a tiny little change, but it was a CHANGE! We had ONE failed cycle with her, and when she saw that it didn't work, she changed it up. I encourage you to take a look at what your RE is doing with your protocol. If you notice that they are not making any changes to it and plan to do the exact same thing again, you have the right to suggest changes. You don't have to know exactly what changes to make, you can simply ask, "Can we try something different?" If they respond with anything other than "Sure" or "Yeah, let's make some changes" or something along those lines, it may be time to look for a new specialist. That's my biggest regret with my own journey. I didn't realize that I had the right to ask for a new protocol.*

At my mid-cycle monitoring appointment, we discovered that I had already ovulated. And I had ovulated three eggs! The doctor sent us home and told us to have sex. Even though I had already ovulated, it appeared that it had recently occurred, so sex was our best bet, and IUI was not an option. We took her advice and had ourselves a good time.

About a week later, I had unusual abdominal pains, different pains than I'd ever experienced. I considered that it might be early pregnancy symptoms, but with so much failure during this journey, it seemed like an impossibility. A few days later, I had some unusual spotting and thought it could be implantation bleeding. After a few more days of feeling different than I'd ever felt, I took a pregnancy test. I said to Dave, "My gut says it's positive, but my head says it's negative." Five minutes later, the test was positive. *It was my very first positive pregnancy test ever.* I was shocked, and I struggled to wrap my mind around what I was seeing. I didn't believe it, but I couldn't *not* believe it either. We were pregnant!

The moment we saw that positive test, we looked at each other, turned bright red and yelled, "WHAT?!" We couldn't believe what we were seeing. We watched each other's' eyes well up with tears and lost our ability to speak momentarily. We were so excited that we quickly rushed to get showered and dressed to head to my in-laws for a pre-Thanksgiving gathering. But our magical moment of happiness was briefly overshadowed by a bloody mess when Dave slipped and fell in the shower, gashing his knee open mere minutes after our positive pregnancy test. We still laugh about the ridiculous turn of events that day.

That week, I had my beta test (pregnancy blood test), and it was positive. My hCG levels were very high, so they scheduled an ultrasound. The ultrasound showed three distinct sacs, confirming that I was pregnant with triplets — **TRIPLETS.** Prior to that moment, I knew in my gut it was triplets. Call it fate, intuition, or psychic ability I didn't know I had! My gut knew what I was about to see, and it was … I'm not sure if there is a word in the English language to accurately describe what I felt in that moment. It was that powerful.

It's enough of a shock to see more than one embryo on an ultrasound, but after 13 failed fertility treatments, seeing three sacs takes it to a whole new level. But that whole new level is compounded even more by my family history of multiples, since my older sister gave birth to spontaneous fraternal twins 13 years earlier. I always thought how cool it would be if I also had twins. As is often the case with my imagination, the excitement of that concept took on a life of its own at that time, and I began dreaming of having triplets. "How crazy would it be if I eventually have triplets someday?"

That was a thought that popped into my mind thousands of times over those 13 years between my nieces being born and that day at the RE's office. I convinced myself that someday, I was going to be a mom of triplets. It was just the way it was going to be. And then **BOOM**, I'm sitting at the doctor's office having my first ever pregnancy ultrasound, and there are three babies living inside my body. It felt like all of the magic and wonder of the universe had come together and was apologizing for the hell it had put me through during my infertility journey.

All three heartbeats were visible the following week, and for the first time, it felt real. I was anxious every day as my RE warned that I could potentially lose one, two, or possibly all three babies. I continued staying positive and talked to my babies daily. I'd tell them how wanted they were and that if they could just hang on, I'd love to be their mommy. I also told them that if they were unable to hold on, I wouldn't be angry. I told them it was okay to let go because the most important thing was for them to do what they needed to do, whatever that may be.

At nine weeks, I miscarried one of the babies. It was by far one of the hardest experiences of my life. I've never been a religious person, and I've never been one to pray or speak to a higher power, but for these babies, I *had* prayed. Every day, I prayed for them to grow inside me and thrive. I'd pray for their future, the chance to get to know them, the chance for them to be born and discover the world. I never expected that I would lose one of them. Though my specialist "prepared" me for this outcome, I was not prepared. It felt like a cruel joke, and I constantly told myself that it wasn't reality. But it *was* my reality.

It was my bizarre and confusing reality as I still had two *other* babies living inside me, and I had to focus on them. It made for a very complicated and difficult grieving process. I'd think about the baby I'd lost, but I couldn't properly grieve because grief takes energy. And that was energy I did not have.

I convinced myself that I didn't need to grieve because I still had two more babies depending on me. I foolishly listened to those who would say, "It was so early in your pregnancy; it hadn't even developed into a baby yet," or, "You should be happy that you still have two other babies!" Except, it was **MY** baby — my baby that I had worked so hard for, that grew in my womb for nine weeks, and that I lost on Christmas Eve. It was my baby that I dreamed about my whole life — my baby.

And I had already experienced a similar loss with my failed IVF. Our growing embryo lived in my womb for a short time, and while it never implanted, it was **MY** baby — my baby that I created with my husband. The pain of that loss was exactly the same as my miscarriage. There's nothing that anyone can ever say to take away the pain of losing your baby. It's painful. It's devastating. It feels like you can't possibly survive.

> *Tip: There's no shame in grieving the loss of your baby. There's no shame in grieving the loss of what you thought your reproductive journey would be. The one thing I*

> *needed at that time was support from a trained professional. Because of the uniqueness of my situation, between infertility, a multiple pregnancy, and a loss of one of three babies, I needed support from someone who could help me navigate the nuances of this situation.*

But ... I *did* survive. I mourned the loss of my babies, and I've never forgotten either of them — my miscarriage and my embryo that didn't implant during IVF. But even with that horrible loss, my IVF loss, my entire infertility journey, and all of the complications in my pregnancy and postpartum period, I survived. And that is the light in all of this darkness — survival.

In the end, it took three years, 14 fertility treatment cycles, a triplet pregnancy, and a miscarriage to get our beloved boy/girl twins whom we treasure so much. My journey wasn't easy — no one's is. But I fought for what I wanted, and eventually, my infertility journey transitioned into a pregnancy journey, and then a postpartum journey. My infertility journey made me stronger and braver than I ever knew I could be. It made me a warrior, and I carry that title proudly.

MORE STORIES OF HELP AND HOPE FOR YOUR JOURNEY

Unlock a special video message from Cara and receive a free gift when you scan this code!

Cara B. Drescher is an infertility coach specializing in helping women navigate and heal from the emotional, physical, and spiritual trauma of infertility and pregnancy/postpartum after infertility. As a former infertility warrior turned mom of twins, she knows firsthand the struggles and long-term effects of infertility. After her own 3-year battle with infertility, Cara conceived triplets and went on to give birth to twins at 32 weeks after a very complicated high-risk pregnancy. When her twins were 8 months old, she realized that her passion for helping people was evolving into a new direction, so she started a podcast and became a coach for women going through infertility. Prior to her career as a coach, Cara was (and still is) a licensed massage therapist, nationally certified continuing education provider, and licensed esthetician specializing in fertility, pregnancy, and postpartum bodywork, skincare, and education. With her 20-plus years of experience in the wellness industry and extensive training in reproductive struggles and successes, Cara brings a unique approach to her coaching style. Lastly, Cara is also an artist. As a textile artist, she designs and sews unique, organization-focused women's wallets using antique and vintage upholstery fabrics. Using her knowledge and continued education of muscular and skin anatomy, aromatherapy, and herbs for topical use, she also creates all natural muscle balms, roll on oils, lip balms, hand soaps, and more.

A VETERAN'S JOURNEY TO CONCEPTION: NAVIGATING INFERTILITY TREATMENT AND RESOURCES WITH THE VA

Courtney Mae Ripoll-McBride

When I was growing up, I don't remember thinking much about having a family in the future. It was always my little brother and me against the world. I do not even remember having parenting goals of how many kids I would have. The transition from the Air Force to civilian life is what made me start to think about this.

After being medically retired from the Air Force, my husband and I started to consider creating a family. When we both left the military, we decided to move from New Mexico to North Dakota. At the time of the move, I was 22. My cycle was always heavy and painful to varying degrees but I thought it was normal. I always thought infertility was for women who were older. Never did I think I would need to explore infertility treatment at age 22, but after two years with no success, we decided to see a doctor. When we started talking to doctors, we were told it was unexplained infertility.

Working with the VA or Veterans Health Administration was an interesting process. The way it worked for me was that I first talked to my primary care doctor about my concerns and asked questions. The main questions were along the lines of what was wrong with me and why I was not getting pregnant when it seemed like some people had no problems. It was a frustrating time for me, and I felt like a failure. It wasn't supposed to be this hard.

I was then informed at my appointment about how the Veterans Health Administration was starting to offer women veterans infertility treatment options. I had no idea this would be an option for us. I was one of the first at our VA to receive infertility treatments.

The way the process worked was that you get a referral outside the VA system from a community doctor via the community care program. Once the referral was approved, the VA helped me book an appointment with the fertility doctor. I was lucky that the doctor I was given traveled every month to the town we lived in, so I did not always have to take the long drive to see him.

When we met our infertility doctor, my husband and I were nervous wrecks. Our doctor started us out with a medication to help stimulate ovulation. It was not successful.

This led to a procedure in which they injected dye into my ovaries. They wanted to ensure my ovaries were in the proper place and the fallopian tubes were open. Our doctor had high hopes and mentioned that everything looked healthy from the ultrasound and scan. Because of this, he wanted to move forward using injections known as follitropin beta injections. This medication was to trigger the eggs to reach their final stage and be ready for fertilization. To receive the injections, we returned to our fertility doctor's clinic. We were nervous and had no clue what the outcome would be.

When I needed meds, I would have to get a paper script to bring to the VA pharmacy, and sometimes, they had to work with other local pharmacies to get the medication since it was very time sensitive. At one point, they had gotten my medication in; however, someone else had started the process, and they had given her my medication by mistake. That was super frustrating and made me want to give up. In my head, I thought to myself that this was obviously a sign it was not meant to be. However, the pharmacy fixed their mistake, and I got the medication I needed later that day.

Looking back now, I can laugh at a part of our story that, at the time, made me so angry. The medication was an injection. I was terrified of needles and asked my spouse to help me. We got everything all set up and ready to go. When he started to inject the medication, he got so nervous, he started laughing uncontrollably. He laughed so hard he couldn't continue with the injection. I got so frustrated that I just grabbed the syringe and gave it to myself. That memory is one that will always stick with me because, looking back, it taught me so much about what I was capable of. I was able to get over my fear of needles, and even though he did not give the injection, he was able to be there supporting me through the treatments.

TIP: Understanding your partner's limitations and being open and honest with each other about them during this journey is so important.

I am extremely lucky my husband was there for me the whole time supporting me and allowed me to vent. I would say that this time definitely strengthened our relationship as it gave us a cause to work toward. It also helped us with our communication. In the beginning, I was frustrated and didn't want to talk about it. He had us sit down and talk through things instead of letting them fester.

The medication you are on during this journey can impact your emotions in ways you can't control or even expect. I learned that having emotions is nothing to be ashamed of. Talking through it helped me put it in the past and cope with the reactions I had.

My husband was there every step of the way, which I am so thankful for. If I had not had that support, I would have wanted to give up before we even began because infertility takes an emotional toll.

After a few unsuccessful rounds of the injections, we did one round of IUI. I was starting to get discouraged at this point in our journey, and we were planning to take a break to see if that would impact anything. We went to the appointment for the IUI, and it was not our normal doctor. It made us feel unsure about how things were going to turn out.

> *TIP: Sometimes, there are unexpected schedule changes; understand that it's okay to voice your concerns and ask questions for clarification.*

After the two week wait period, we experienced another emotional rollercoaster. I took a urine test at my primary doctor's office and was told it was negative. Earlier in the day, the fertility doctor had told us it was positive. Because of the confusion, the primary doctor had me come back in to have blood drawn. It came back positive. I can honestly tell you that when I saw the positive test, I was in denial. I know part of it was the fact that I got two different answers from two different doctors. Even though I wanted it to be positive more than anything, I was in disbelief. I went through the mini stages of grief for life as I knew it. That may seem strange, but looking back, I was on a lot of hormone medications.

I was on the phone with the doctor confirming the pregnancy when my husband came home; the minute he walked in, I whispered, "I'm pregnant." My husband didn't believe me; I think he said something along the lines of, "Are you sure?"

After being told the test result was negative so many times, it just didn't feel real. Once we saw the ultrasound confirming we were for sure having a child, reality kicked in for both of us. He built her first crib, and I got her room ready to go.

> *TIP: One thing I wish I knew was that no matter what your reaction or emotions are, they are yours. How you move on from your emotions is what matters. What you think and feel does not make you a bad person. Everyone has doubts, and that is okay. We tend to judge ourselves harder than anyone else.*

With a lot of the processes in the VA or any other doctor offices, there are hoops you have to jump through to move to the next step. It can get frustrating and discouraging. One thing to remember is that you have the right to advocate for yourself and fight for the end goal; in my case, it was getting pregnant.

A few weeks after the good news, I thought I had morning sickness. Some of my favorite meals just did not sit right, and everything started to come back up, even water. This was definitely not morning sickness as I understood it. As the pregnancy progressed, it got worse. I was in and out of the ER, receiving IV fluids for the first two or three months of my pregnancy.

When I met with the doctor, I was given IV fluids and Zofran, a medication to help with the nausea. We finally got a diagnosis — hyperemesis gravidarum. This condition shaped me in a big way. I lost around 40 pounds over the course of my pregnancy. I needed a PICC line (an IV that stayed in my arm all the time) and medication to be able to function.

Prior to my PICC line being placed, I was sent to the infusion center for IV fluids and Zofran three times a week. While this was an hour-plus drive there and back, it was one of the most welcoming centers I have ever gone to. I was miserable and nauseous when I showed up, but they always knew how to get a smile out of me.

One of the things that made me smile was the name of the IV fluid bag. It was called a "banana bag" and was most often used for hangovers.

They told me I had to stay until I got some food down. I don't fully recall what I ate there, maybe mashed potatoes, peas and corn, mac 'n cheese, or vegetable soup. I was able to keep down most meals I ate there, and at that time, it was some of the best food I had eaten. This brought the entire nursing staff on that floor pure joy. Some days, on my drive, I'd even ponder what I was going to attempt to eat that day, hoping for a good day; even the nurses would ask if we were going to have a good day that day.

> *TIP: If you are going through HG or something similar, find your "safe" foods. These are foods you can tolerate for the most part and keep down longer than others.*

The amount of care I received was incredible. My doctor or his nurses contacted me weekly to ensure I was okay. Even after the PICC line was placed, they had me come to the infusion center for the next couple of weeks to ensure I was comfortable flushing my own PICC line, connecting the IV bag, and ensuring the pump was running. If I wasn't comfortable, they guided me through every step. After that, I no longer needed the infusion center. That was a bittersweet moment. I had gotten to know the nurses on a personal level, and they felt like a part of my pregnancy.

For the next couple weeks, I had in-home nurses come to help set up my home equipment, allowing me to administer my Zofran and IV fluids in the comfort of my house. I had an allergic reaction to some of the common latex bandages they utilized for PICC lines. The entire staff went above and beyond to find a bandage with the least amount of irritation. Having my bandage replaced was such a relief after having my PICC line for seven to eight months.

While there were some pain points with the PICC line, it also gave me some freedom by being able to administer the IV fluids and Zofran at home. I had the opportunity to go out and run errands, attend quilting events that I enjoyed, and pick-up last-minute items for our little one.

I remember one day quite well. I got stuck in my car, and I was in total panic wondering what I was going to do. My IV line got hung up on the passenger's seat where I could not reach. I had to wait for my husband to get home, so he could help me get out.

In addition to my HG, my pregnancy was nine months of not knowing what was going to happen because I never felt my daughter kick. Because I never felt her, toward the end of my pregnancy, we started non-stress tests to monitor the baby. The night before we started the non-stress tests, I vividly remember feeling like I heard a loud thump. My husband had just fallen asleep, and I jumped up, almost in shock. It was as if I had *heard* our daughter kick, but I did not feel anything.

The non-stress test offered me some peace of mind. The test allowed us to hear the baby's heartbeat. I was stressed between the tests as I felt unsure that everything was okay. It was weird seeing the monitor of her "movements" but not feeling anything.

One day, during our weekly non-stress tests, there was a heartbeat but no movement. They used a little device that would buzz and usually make her move. However, it was not working on my stubborn little one. We had an ultrasound to make sure everything was okay. I was an emotional wreck until they were able to confirm she was okay. The staff was calm and collected throughout and even tried to make me smile while waiting for the ultrasound.

While everyone's journey with hyperemesis gravidarum is different, I consider the level of symptoms I had to be a blessing. I did not have to have a nasogastric tube placed for nutrients like some who have hyperemesis gravidarum. I like to say my daughter was brought to you by my favorite soft drink — IV fluids and Zofran. Many of my friends and family joked that my little one practically stole everything I was able to keep down.

True to the course of the pregnancy, my birth experience was also NOT what I expected. My ideal birth was a water birth. The hospital has amazing bathtubs that I was hoping to labor in. Sadly, when it came time for one of my last exams, my doctor noticed my pelvic floor was tilted and, for the safety of our daughter, recommended a planned C-section at 39 weeks, 1 day.

There were multiple factors that led to my doctor recommending a C-section. He was concerned I wasn't getting enough nutrients, especially being sick 24/7 and on IV fluids and Zofran three times a week. The weekly NST scans were unpredictable, and they often ended with me having an ultrasound to ensure everything was okay.

During her birth, I vividly remember trying to peek over the curtain. I was curious and just wanted to see what was going on. The next thing you know, my doctor swiftly moved my hands back and pulled the curtain even higher up. My doctor was amazing and very supportive. Knowing I did not want narcotics, I ended up having a nerve block done after my incision was closed. He came back and held my hand through the rough part. I will never forget that kindness. In the end, I had my daughter a few weeks after turning 24 and my husband turning 28.

Recovery took a little longer for me, and having the nerve block slowed my progress of being able to get up and walk about. My legs were practically numb, but I had no pain.

> *TIP: Advocate for what you want. I chose no narcotics and asked for options prior to birth. Educate yourself on what the options are before making your decision.*

After my C-section, in the transition to my room, it was a shock for me to be told to start with ice chips and water, since both made me completely sick during my pregnancy. I was extremely hesitant, and tears rolled down my cheeks as I willed myself not to get sick from them. I actually sent my husband out to get me the one meal I craved — Jaeger schnitzel and spaetzle. We'd found a German pub in town prior to getting pregnant. It has one of the best schnitzels I've had; even my husband agreed, and he'd lived in Germany for four years. I missed eating some of my favorite foods while pregnant, and this meal was definitely one of the best I'd had in nine months.

As we got settled in our room after the birth, I attempted to breastfeed. It did not go well at all. I found it to be very painful and frustrating. I tried pumping, but that was not working either. I ended up getting upset and began feeling like a failure again. Eventually, we decided to push back on being told to keep trying and fed our daughter formula. I remember one thing someone told me after the fact that made me feel better. It was, "being fed is better than what people are judging you for." I would rather the baby be fed with formula than not get enough breast milk. I am glad we decided to go for formula and not keep trying to make something happen that was painful and not working.

> *TIP: Knowing what's healthy for you and your child is more important than any judgment you may receive; being fed is best.*

When it was time to go home, my husband left me at the front of the hospital while bringing the car around. That right there scared me. I felt as if we were being kicked out. I'll never forget our first night home. Still in pain from my C-section, my husband and I slept on the couch and our little one in her bassinet. I vividly remember waking up throughout the first night to ask my husband to check on our daughter. Both of us were delirious, running on fumes, and half asleep. Once, I asked my husband where our daughter was, as he had handed me a rolled-up blanket without her in it, insisting it was her. Both of us were in disarray and full-blown panic as we searched for her, only to find out she was still in her bassinet, ready for some food and a fresh diaper.

The first night, and many others, I could hardly sleep, and I was always checking my daughter's breathing. Because of my anxiety, we ended up investing in a sock that would check her heart rate and oxygen levels. Even with the sock monitoring her, I would still wake up; however, it was not as often.

Postpartum depression was a journey of healing in itself. There is so much I wish I had known back then.

At the time, I did not have a label for how I was feeling. Through my pregnancy, I was seeing a therapist, and I continued with her after birth. I started going to therapy for my postpartum depression, and opening up with my therapist really helped. Originally, I did not talk much about my feelings; however, after I became more comfortable, I opened up about how I was feeling. I was reluctant to share my feelings at first as they made me feel like a failure.

> *TIP: Don't be afraid to talk about what you are going through. I wish I had talked about it more at the time.*

Looking back, I wish I talked about more with those around me to build up the community aspect. I wish I understood that I didn't have to do it on my own with just my spouse. No one should have to go through it alone. Know it's okay to talk; know when you need help. Remove that thought of judgment and know that no one is going to judge you for seeking help; everyone deserves to find that little help when needed.

What really helped me a lot with my anxiety and how I was feeling was having my daughter with me. Having a sense of clarity being with her brought a sense of understanding, knowing that everything was going to be okay with my daughter.

> *TIP: One thing I wish I had known is that everyone's feelings are different; it is okay to feel what you're feeling. Know that reaching out for help doesn't make you a failure.*

Infertility shaped me as a parent in many ways. One major way is that anytime my daughter is sick, I become an anxious mess. I check her temperature and breathing obsessively. Now that she is a bit older, she swats the thermometer away. She is our one and only child. Not knowing or not being in control of the situation really gets to me when it comes to her being sick. I would like to think that if I did not have this journey, I might not have picked this quirk up or taken it to this extreme.

Throughout this entire wild journey of infertility, hyperemesis gravidarum, C-section, and postpartum issues with all the unexpected turns, I realized that none of us are alone in this — whether you dealt with infertility for years, you were unsuccessful throughout multiple rounds of treatment, you experienced hyperemesis gravidarum, or you had complications during pregnancy or birth. Building your community and having those loved ones to talk through your struggles can really strengthen you as a whole to be there for your loved ones and your little bundle of joy.

MORE STORIES OF HELP AND HOPE FOR YOUR JOURNEY

Unlock a special video message from Courtney and receive a free gift when you scan this code!

Courtney Mae is a hyperemesis gravidarum survivor, loving wife, and mother of one special daughter. Outside of being a mother, business owner, podcast host, and pursuing her MBA with a concentration in project management, Courtney Mae loves spending time with her family watching their favorite TV shows, quilting, and reading.

MORE TITLES AVAILABLE ON AMAZON

Want to connect with one of the authors of Infertility Success, MORE Stories? Scan Here to connect

BONUS CHAPTERS FROM
Infertility Success, Stories of Help and Hope for Your Journey

TO HELL AND BACK: A JOURNEY TO MOTHERHOOD

Susan Tozer

"I'm going to tell you something that is going to blow your mind."

Those words still haunt me. Whenever I hear the words "blow your mind," I am taken back to that day in Dr. V.'s office. The 10th of December, 2009, the day our dream of starting a family shattered into a million sharp, heart-piercing pieces.

After my husband and I got married in October, 2001, at the age of 24, we decided to wait before starting a family. We were young and wanted to see the world. If only we knew how precious those years would prove to be. At age 27, we decided we might be ready to start a family. Our mindset was that if it happens, it happens. At that stage, I was very naïve and ignorant about fertility. We stopped all contraception and started "making babies."

We were ecstatic to find out at Christmas 2006 that we were pregnant, two years after we had stopped contraception. I never thought to do the math because we were in no hurry to conceive. We were living in England at the time and travelling Europe.

> *Tip: Consider seeking help to conceive if you are younger than 35 and have been trying to conceive for at least a year or if you're 35 or older and have been trying to conceive for at least 6 months. Seek help from a medical professional specializing in fertility. Do not hesitate to go for second or third opinions.*

Throughout my twenties, I only had regular periods while I was taking oral contraceptives. Without them, my periods were erratic and varied in length. I never knew when to expect it.

At the end of January, 2007, our world fell apart for the first time when I had a miscarriage. We were about ten weeks along. We nicknamed the baby "Beanie" early in the pregnancy, and that is what we have always called him. I say 'him' because, in my heart, I have always thought of him as a boy.

We heard the usual ignorant comments like "at least it happened early," "hopefully the next one sticks," "you're still young; you can try again," "there was obviously something wrong with it." 'It' was our baby, and we didn't want a different baby. We already loved him.

Now what? Do we just wake up the next morning and continue with our lives as if nothing had happened? No funeral? No flowers or sympathy cards?

I gritted my teeth, tried to push the feelings down, and got on with life. "There was hardly a baby there. Stop feeling sorry for yourself. Other people have gone through much worse," I'd tell myself.

INFERTILITY SUCCESS

> *Tip: Allow yourself time to grieve a loss. Seek counseling or at least a supportive, understanding person to speak to. Ignoring the emotions or blaming yourself delays healing.*

I thought I had done something to cause the miscarriage. I thought perhaps I wasn't meant to be a mother, that maybe I wouldn't be a good enough mother. Deep down, I knew there was something wrong with my body. I had a gut feeling for a long time. Something wasn't right.

Over the next two years, I wasted many hours seeing doctors who thought they knew about fertility. They dismissed me and told me nothing was wrong. "Make an appointment for blood tests on the second day of your next period," they'd suggest. How? With these erratic periods, I don't know when the second day will be. "You don't ovulate regularly. Just make sure you have intercourse every second day." Sounds easy, doesn't it? Sounds like fun, doesn't it? It made me feel like we weren't trying hard enough. Maybe we were "doing it" wrong.

The lab messed up my husband's sperm analysis results and wrote in large, red letters "LOW MOTILITY." Dr. V. would later discard that piece of paper with the remark, "Based on what?!". It turned out, my husband's swimmers were perfectly fine.

I believed all the ridiculous things people say. "Relax, you're thinking about it too much." "If you go on holiday/move house/get a new job/pray harder, you will fall pregnant." I tried all those things. In the meantime, my friends were having their first or second children.

Back home in South Africa, in June, 2009, we decided it was time to seek help from a fertility specialist.

The fertility clinic did a full work up on both of us. At the initial scan, Dr. V. shook his head and said, "These ovaries are very quiet." I didn't know what that meant. I do now.

While waiting for the test results, I thought they would tell me I'd need to use the drug Clomid, which I had heard helped so many friends of my friends fall pregnant. Worst case scenario, I thought we'd have to do IVF. I spent time reading up a lot on fertility treatments, joined an online forum for women struggling to conceive, and somewhere along the way, I read an article on women making use of egg donors. "How wonderful," I thought. "Perhaps I'll donate some of my eggs once we've had our babies."

One day in December, 2009, Dr. V. called and requested to see us immediately. I knew then that something was very wrong. I got some numbers out of him on the phone, entered it into a search engine online, found an article, sank down onto my knees, and started sobbing. Please, no. Please, God, don't do this to us. Thankfully, I was working at home. I hoped that I had misunderstood what I had read. We went to see Dr. V. the next day. He entered the office, and in his soft-spoken, serious manner, said, "I'm going to tell you something that is going to blow your mind."

What I had read online was true. I was 32 years old, had hardly any eggs left, and those I did have were of terrible quality. It's called premature ovarian failure (POF). I had a very high FSH (follicle-stimulating hormone) level, nearly undetectable AMH (anti-Müllerian hormone) level, and very low antral follicle count. Dr. V. told us that our chances of conceiving naturally were extremely low, and if successful, chances of miscarriage were quite high. I had "the ovaries of a fifty-year-old." He said that, of course, it's not impossible that we could conceive naturally and carry a healthy baby to term, and should this happen, he would be the first to congratulate us.

> *Tip: Premature ovarian failure (POF), also known as primary ovarian insufficiency (POI), is a loss of ovarian function before the age of 40. POF can affect women from their teenage years to their thirties. Women with POF are at a greater risk of a range of health issues, including osteoporosis, estrogen deficiency, and heart diseases. The loss of ovarian function means that the probability of a woman falling pregnant with her own eggs is greatly reduced.*

Dr. V. told us the best chance we had of conceiving and carrying a baby to term was using donor eggs (DE). He explained that I could expect to go into menopause early. It was a massive shock. I tried to ask questions between sobs. My husband was stunned and trying to make sense of exactly what we were up against. He asked whether it would be worth trying an IVF cycle with my eggs. Dr. V. responded that we could try, of course, but that the cycle could be cancelled because I wouldn't respond well enough to the medication. He said that he wouldn't, in good conscience, suggest an IVF cycle with my eggs and take our money.

I couldn't understand how this could be possible. Was it something I did? Was I being punished by God for something? I couldn't think of anything I could have done that could possibly warrant this punishment and pain. Rapists, paedophiles, and murderers get to have children. Even flies have babies!

We were devastated. My husband cried and said, "I don't want another woman's babies. I want your babies." My heart broke again at that. I had to go through a grieving process and a lot of therapy to come to terms with the idea of using another woman's eggs and my potential child not having my genes. Would I be able to bond with this child? Would they one day reject me as not being their "real mom"? I was ashamed and embarrassed. I felt like I wasn't a real woman. I offered to help my husband find a better, proper, fertile wife. He wasn't impressed with that suggestion at all. I hated my body. I hated myself. I was broken, less than, old, barren.

We looked for a donor that had the same physical features as me, someone we felt a connection with while reading her profile. It felt weird, like shopping for an egg carrier. In South Africa, egg donation is anonymous – unless you use a family member or friend who offers to donate her eggs. I armed myself with information and made learning everything I could about this condition and process my new mission in life.

> *Tip: Everyone has different things they look for in a donor profile. What helped me was to imagine myself writing a donor profile. Would someone pick me? It is not possible to find a perfect, cardboard cut-out woman.*

We jumped in and then … that first DE IVF attempt didn't work.

This was 2010. We went through this process another six times with another five donors.

Read donor profiles. Choose a donor. Wait for a period to start. Start oral contraceptives – because that's how we get pregnant. Wait for the donor to start her period and take all her meds. Go for scans. Pray. Beg. Cry. Hope. Wait for news on the egg retrieval. Wait for the fertilization report. Wait for day 5. Another embryo transfer. Another excruciating two week wait. Another negative pregnancy test. More tears. More screaming into a pillow in rage. Lots of therapy. Perfecting a fake smile. Picking myself up off the floor. Putting one foot in front of the other. Working hard to earn money for the next attempt. Lots of wine. Rinse and repeat.

With each attempt, we'd tweak something. Slightly different meds, ZIFT (zygote intrafallopian transfer), intralipids, and so on. There was no explanation as to why it wasn't working. There seemed to be nothing else wrong with my body. After the ZIFT, Dr. V. confirmed that my ovaries looked like raisins.

My husband would read donor profiles and make spreadsheets for me, listing the characteristics of each donor. I would then make a shortlist and read those profiles before we decided on one together.

Along the way, donors we had selected were rejected for hereditary conditions, concerns over hormone levels, and dishonesty. I could try to describe every attempt, but it all became a bit of a blur, and the worst was yet to come.

> *Tip: Arm yourself with as much information as you can. Take questions and a notepad along to consultations. It is often a lot of information to take in.*

I hated it when people said that it would "happen in God's time." If someone would just tell me when that time would be, then I could get on with my life until that time arrived. I hated that four-letter word 'just.' 'Just' adopt, 'just' use a surrogate, 'just' relax.

At some point, Dr. V. mentioned surrogacy. We went to a presentation on surrogacy with an open mind but decided against it. Everyone has a line, and that was ours. I couldn't face watching another woman carry my baby.

The final suggestion Dr. V. made was regression therapy because, as he conveyed to me in an email:

"I believe there are deeper issues, issues that neither you, me nor Raymond are aware of, that inhibit conception and prevent us from having the outcome that we want. Quantum physics literature is clear on the fact that 'if the vessel is not 100% sound', meaning not just physically, but at a deeply emotional level, that nothing positive will happen in that vessel, but that a spiral will start that will continue to spiral downwards until the issue/s are resolved. There are countless examples of couples not being able to conceive due to *a deep-seated emotional issue* that prevents this from happening. I believe this may be the case in your instance."

He referred me to a clinical psychologist specializing in regression therapy via hypnosis, Dr. O. We were very surprised and a little sceptical about this. Until then, we hadn't met a medical professional that had a holistic perspective. We decided to trust Dr. V. since we didn't have another plan anyway.

And so, in 2012, I started down a path straight through hell, a path that would change me forever and, after which, I'd need therapy for many years to come.

> *Tip: Therapy to deal with trauma is invaluable. There is great benefit in having someone that is not emotionally involved help you to process the feelings around the trauma that you suffered, regardless of how 'big' the trauma was.*

Hypnotherapy is not what you might have seen on television, where a person is made to cluck like a chicken, apparently without knowing what they're doing. I can describe it as what happens when you're driving a car, deep inside a memory, not completely focusing on the road, and suddenly, a dog runs in front of your car. Immediately, you are back to the present time, slamming your foot down on the brake. You were present, yet not quite.

I went into the process thinking that, deep down, I believed that I wouldn't be a good enough mother or that I didn't deserve to be a mother. There were some sessions during which it felt like we hardly made any progress. We started off exploring my childhood, my birth, my parenting, and at some point, Dr. O. asked me to visualize what my womb looks like. I saw a black, sludgy pool bubbling with poison. We had to discover why it looked like that. Through a few hellish sessions, I discovered that I had been repeatedly sexually abused by a family member that used to babysit me. In the worst incident, I heard what I can only describe as my soul screaming. It was incredibly traumatic. I remember thinking, at the time, that this must be what hell feels like. I often wanted to give up, but I needed to see this through if I was to heal and fulfill our dream of having a child.

Next, I had to, under hypnosis, fix the damage to my womb, to clean out all the poison. By the middle of 2013, I felt healed enough to continue with the next DE IVF cycle.

The monster that abused me died at the end of 2013. That little girl was now free and safe at last.

Our last attempt with DE IVF was at the start of 2014. I was done looking for a donor. Done reading profiles. I insisted (i.e., asked very nicely) that the clinic find a donor for us. We couldn't care less what she looked like, so long as it worked. The only physical characteristics we had in common was our height and the shape of our noses. This was it. We had reached the end of our tether. In that last cycle, we did things differently. We decided to spend the two-week wait for the results on holiday at the coast rather than trying to stay busy at work. I like to joke that I went on holiday and came back pregnant, like everyone said I should do.

Our beautiful daughter was born in November, 2014, after a relatively easy pregnancy. She is feisty, assertive, strong-willed, and utterly adorable.

And you know what? It doesn't matter one iota to me that she doesn't have my genes. Genetics isn't what makes a family. If any of those other cycles had worked, we wouldn't have had this child. Yes, we might have had someone else, but not her, and we cannot imagine our life without her. I know we were meant to be together. Infertility and fertility treatment is no walk in the park, and it costs a fortune, but in the end, the journey was worth every cent we spent and every tear we shed.

We are forever grateful to our donor, whomever and wherever she is, for the enormous gift she has given us. She didn't just give us some eggs. She gave us a lifetime of memories and firsts. First birthday, first tooth, first laugh, first steps, first words, first "I love you, mommy," first tantrum, first day of school, and all the other normal things that parents experience.

> *Tip: Make self-care a priority. Not 'soft' self-care in the shape of candle-lit bubble baths, but 'messy' self-care in the form of being selective who you share information with, putting yourself first, and strong boundaries. Start cultivating healthy coping mechanisms and methods of stress relief. If possible, join a support group – in person or online. I found talk therapy to be invaluable. PPD and/or PTSD is prevalent among infertile women using ART (assisted reproductive technology) to conceive.*

INFERTILITY SUCCESS

Unlock a special video message from Susan and receive a free gift when you scan this code!

Susan Tozer has lived a life that people write novels about. Now she is taking pen to paper to do just that herself. From miscarriage to infertility and so much more, Susan brings her wit and charm to her brutally honest and refreshing stories.

By day Susan works as a software developer, and in her spare time can be found fighting dragons or catching unicorns with her much dreamed of daughter. Susan's other passion lies in helping infertile women like herself find solace and companionship and enlightening the public on infertility.

SEVEN DIAGNOSES AND SEVEN YEARS TO FOUR SONS

Erica Hoke

If ever there was a woman that was least likely to conceive, it was me. I was over age 35 when I was diagnosed with stage four endometriosis, uterine fibroids, PCOS, thyroid disease, low ferritin, low ovarian reserve, and factor 5 leiden. With seven contributing infertility diagnoses, I was still considered to have "unexplained infertility." In the back of my mind, IVF was a choice of last resort, or at least it was a choice... until it wasn't.

My husband and I sat in the reproductive endocrinologist office. "You're 35, and you're already hyper-ovulating. Your body is already doing the job that medicine we give you would do. The ultrasound and bloodwork show you have very few eggs left."

"I'm sorry," he said. "You have a better chance of hitting the lottery than getting pregnant." The only option the REI could offer us was IUI, which carried a less than five percent chance of success. Those odds weren't good enough for us, especially since, at that point, we knew my husband's swimmers were "Olympic" level. That's when I started researching anything and everything that affects fertility and then implementing these changes.

> TIP: If you're given a poor prognosis with few choices, get another opinion.

That "no" to IVF treatment from our REI wasn't the beginning of our journey. We had been traveling a path to find answers and heal my body from my many reproductive diagnoses for several years. But to understand the full picture, you have to know that my problems started a few years after my first period.

The first memory of the intensity of my periods increasing was Thanksgiving. I rushed from the table to throw up and spent the day in bed. At sixteen, just three years after starting my period, this was "normal" for the first day of my cycle.

The gynecologist offered a prescription for an NSAID and the platitude that the pain was "normal."

> TIP: Extreme period pain that includes vomiting, an inability to stand upright, or causes you to miss school or work is not normal and requires additional investigation to determine the medical root cause.

Years later, I was able to see the pattern of what I believed caused the disease that took doctors 15 years to diagnose.

I met my husband one day on a sales call for my job. We were both divorced with no children. When we met, we were both in our early to mid-30s. As our relationship progressed and we spent more time together, he was able to see first-hand what I dealt with on a monthly basis.

Over the 15+ years of having my period, I dealt with the pain mostly by being on hormonal birth control. Convinced this was causing a lot of other symptoms, I decided to stop using it. I was concerned about the long-term effects on my fertility and determined to get my body in the best possible health to carry a baby.

Within months of stopping the pill, my pain had increased to an excruciating level. I was working in outside sales, and my flow was nearly impossible to manage. During a networking lunch, I met a traditional Chinese medicine doctor who practiced acupuncture and would change the course of my life. She assured me that she could help me. It seemed like as soon as I found help, my body went on attack. More than once, my then-boyfriend had to deliver me to her office for treatment while I was sobbing and unable to stand.

In addition to acupuncture, my new gynecologist, although amazing, was ethically bound to only be able to tell me my symptoms *could be* endometriosis or uterine fibroids. Diagnosis meant surgery. Eventually, unable to get relief, I sought out a surgeon who specializes in endometriosis. I was terrified the surgery would cause scarring in my uterus that would prevent me from getting pregnant.

> *TIP: If your doctor suspects endometriosis or uterine fibroids,* **don't delay** *confirming the diagnosis with surgery. DO find a surgeon that will diagnose AND perform the surgical excision at the same surgery.*

We discussed what would happen if she found endometriosis. She let me know that she was one of the few surgeons who would perform the laparoscopic surgery *and* perform the excision surgery. After lots of talking it over and consideration, I decided to have the surgery.

When I woke up from the surgery, the surgeon said she removed *a lot* of endometrioses, stage 4 endometriosis, to be exact. It was the diagnosis I had been waiting 15 years for. It was both inside and outside of my uterus, attached to my ovaries, bladder, and bowels. She was able to see I also had PCOS.

She felt confident that, because of her aggressive surgery, most, if not all, of my problems would be over. She was wrong. While grateful for her skill as a surgeon, the next few months would be some of the most trying of my journey up until that point.

> *TIP: Before any surgical procedure, any doctor should complete a basic blood panel to confirm your overall health.*

Bleeding was to be expected for a few weeks following the surgery, but when a month went by, and my bleeding hadn't stopped, I contacted the surgeon. She sent me home with no suggestions and a "wait and see" attitude. The pain was gone, but for the next 90+ days, I had period-like flow. Little did I know, I was literally bleeding to death.

> *TIP: If any doctor tells you they can't help you with a problem that seems concerning to you or is disruptive to your life, get a second opinion or keep doing your own research until you find an answer.*

I was back to work full time, but I was exhausted. I went to work and came home and headed straight for the couch. Around this time, I drove out of town for work. When I got to the event, I had so much pain in my leg that I couldn't walk. Something was wrong.

A few days later, a red, belt strap looking welt appeared on my leg. I went to see my doctor. After some discussion and hesitation, he decided to send me to the hospital for the ultrasound I didn't receive days earlier when I visited the ER. The ultrasound was inconclusive, and I was admitted to the hospital.

I was so afraid and freaked out. At 33, I was being admitted to the hospital for the first time. The doctor ordered blood work and blood thinners "just in case" I had a blood clot in my leg. A nurse came in to get my blood thinners started, and I was making small talk with her when a tiny voice in my head sounded an alarm.

> *TIP: If you have an intuition about something or feel something is off, trust your instinct. Always confirm and ask to see any medication being given to you in the hospital.*

I looked over at the tray **full** of small vials she was steadily pushing into my IV. I asked, *"Are you going to give me all of that?"* It was a question that saved my life. She looked at me and told me that she would be right back. I never saw her again during my 10-day hospital stay. Instead, a male nurse bustled into the room with an IV pole with a bag of vitamin K hung on it, the antidote to blood thinners.

I had been overdosed by a whole decimal point. Had I not noticed, my organs and brain would have liquefied before the antidote could have been administered.

The lab results revealed that I had a gene mutation called factor 5 leiden. According to a local geneticist, up to 80% of the population is a carrier. If not diagnosed, it leads to chemical pregnancy, miscarriage, still birth, and secondary infertility. Ultimately, this diagnosis would allow me to go on to hold and carry my pregnancies. Along with this diagnosis came hope.

> *Tip: If you have had even one miscarriage, or suspect chemical pregnancies, get tested for a blood clotting panel, especially factor 5 leiden.*

In addition, I also had an undiagnosed thyroid issue causing my continuous bleeding from the surgery. Because of my blood loss, my red blood count was 2 points away from being fatal.

Diagnosed and back on the road to health with my now-fiancé, I knew that I still had some problems to solve. The endometriosis surgery had eliminated most (but not all) of my pain but not the torrential flow that became the norm. I sought out our town's only reproductive endocrinologist that specializes in infertility to get recommendations on next steps. He recommended my gynecologist perform a laparoscopic surgery to determine/remove any fibroids he could see.

The laparoscopic surgery was unsuccessful. My OB/GYN couldn't see a single fibroid to remove. Seeing my anguish, he let me know that there might be another type of fibroid surgery that could be done by the REI to be certain that I didn't have any fibroids. He explained that when looking into the uterus, the fibroids might be receding into the wall of the uterus. A saline infusion sonogram would allow the surgeon to see the fibroids better.

Bounced back to my REI, I scheduled the surgery as soon as I could. I was willing to do whatever it took to get to the bottom of my pain. When I woke up, I was shocked by the news the surgeon had for me.

Not only did he find that I DID, in fact, have fibroids, he removed so many that it looked like a handful of aquarium gravel. I was horrified because all that I could think about was whether or not each fibroid scar would be one less piece of real estate in my uterus but also thrilled because I was hopeful that this meant I would be pain-free.

Now, with the endo and fibroids gone, I *was sure* we were on a short path to parenthood. One month went by and then two. I was pain-free and having normal cycles now but more concerned than ever about the ticking clock and no pregnancy.

Now that my problems were cleared up, I started to question if something could be wrong with my husband. No one ever suggested my husband be tested for male factor infertility.

> *TIP: Request as much testing up front as you can. Even if you have to pay out of pocket for it. Don't wait (for time, miscarriages, or failed IVF/IUI) to start procedures/testing. Don't wait to test your partner until issues with you are ruled out.*

My husband got a glowing report on his swimmers, and we were back to the drawing board.

During our next two week wait, we decided to splurge and take a combined birthday/anniversary trip to Disney to relax and take a break from all thing's fertility-related (at least the painful ones). We ate a lot of good food, drank a lot of good wine, and then, at Epcot, got on the world's largest centrifuge (in the form of the ride Mission Space).

When we returned home, I went straight to acupuncture treatment. Afterward, Dr. H. and I decided to attend a chamber of commerce function. As we were walking around the different tables, she reached over to grab my hand and feel my pulse. She stopped dead in her tracks and turned to face me squarely, still gripping my wrist. "You're pregnant! and it's a boy!"

"What?!" I say, "I haven't even taken a pregnancy test." It was several more days of waiting before I was brave enough to confirm the prediction. We WERE pregnant and over the moon with excitement! It was my first positive pregnancy test ever.

Once the pregnancy was confirmed and the blood thinners on board to prevent a clot, we went about our business in the manner of any new and excited parents. I continued to work and, although monitored very closely, didn't have any scares, minus some spotting during an out-of-town business trip. It was a perfectly uneventful pregnancy.

We welcomed our first son after a 28-hour labor prevented him from being born on Christmas Day. I was 36.

After 15 months with a *super easy* baby, we were convinced that we were genius parents and ready to expand our family. We knew from the start that we wanted as many children as the Lord would allow us to have.

We returned to the same REI (in hindsight, I'm not sure why), and he had an even bleaker prognosis for us. After two and a half years, my blood work, including my AMH, was terrible. When he looked at my follicle count via ultrasound, he declared that I would need donor eggs in order to conceive. I think we were both stunned with disbelief.

My husband and I never even talked about using donor eggs as an option. Instead, we decided to drive an hour away for a second opinion. Unfortunately, this doctor wasn't any more optimistic about my outcome. He *did*, however, suggest that I take the blood thinners that I would need during pregnancy before we got a positive pregnancy test. He handed me a prescription and sent us on our way. It was Tuesday, and we were in our two week wait window.

Friday, I woke up feeling optimistic enough to take an early test. Much to my surprise, it was positive!!!! I couldn't believe my eyes. I rushed to the pharmacy to fill my prescription and schedule an ultrasound with my doctor.

While I was caring for our not quite two-year-old and waiting for the ultrasound, my husband noticed that I often referred to the pregnancy as "they" or "them." Hmm. That's weird, I thought. I wonder why I'm doing that? Both my husband and I had prophetic dreams about having twin girls.

Finally, it was ultrasound day, and we relayed our suspicions to the doctor. "Nope, just one baby here." We weren't disappointed and just blew it off. We were happily pregnant again.

I was very sick very early in the pregnancy. I had an ultrasound scheduled, but my husband stayed home (the only ultrasound he ever missed) with our son, who had the sniffles. The doctor placed the ultrasound wand on my stomach, and as the screen lit up, there were two "fried egg" images on the screen. It was the top of both my sons' heads. "That looks like twins!" I said. "It sure does!" he replied. Our prediction was correct.

Our twin boys were born at 39 weeks, 27 months after the birth of their big brother, one vaginally and one via c-section. I wouldn't change a thing about the outcome of our birth experience. Happy as a family of five, we struggled through our first year of twin life and then hit our stride the second year.

One morning, one of the boys woke me up. We had just returned from vacation, and my husband was gone on a business trip. The night before, I'd realized that I lost track of my period, and I reminded myself that when one of the boys woke in the morning, I would take a pregnancy test I had left over, "just in case." I peed on the stick, set it aside, and went to care for my son, almost forgetting on my way back to bed that I hadn't looked at it.

I was unconcerned, after all of our previous tracking, that this could be a "surprise" pregnancy. After all, I was 41. I flipped on the light and was STUNNED to see two dark lines staring back at me. We were pregnant! WOW. The birth would be the exact same spacing as the first two. Twenty-seven months.

The pregnancy was problematic from the start. First of all, it was the Friday before Labor Day weekend. I phoned the office as soon as they opened to make sure I got my blood thinner medicine before the weekend. It didn't happen. They closed at noon. It would be late the following week before they could see me.

Despite my panic, I tried to tell myself that it would be okay. I was wrong. By the time I was seen for my first appointment, they couldn't detect a heartbeat. They sent me to the hospital for a second detailed ultrasound, and I learned that I miscarried not one but two babies. We will always feel like that was our twin girls.

The miscarriage was devastating. Busy with the boys and convinced that another pregnancy was out of the question, we gave accidental pregnancy very little thought. Now, we were determined this miscarriage would not be how our story ended.

Months passed and then the year anniversary of the miscarriage. I was 42 and needed surgery to correct a severe diastasis rectus from the twin's pregnancy (combined, I carried over 12 pounds of baby) that left me looking five months pregnant on my size 4 frame.

We set a deadline of January 1st, 2015, to stop trying. I would be 43 that year and needed closure. I had given up hope. Seventeen months after the loss of our twins, and just two days before our "deadline," we got our positive pregnancy test!

After another uneventful pregnancy, I delivered, via unmedicated VBAC, our last son. It was truly a redemptive experience. We call him our 11th hour baby.

We welcomed our fourth son **SEVEN** years after medical professionals told us that we would not be able to conceive on our own or would need donor eggs. There are a lot of procedures/surgeries and details I was not able to include here due to space constraints. Some of these include massive changes in my diet, including switching to organic proteins, then organic veggies, then low/no processed foods. I eliminated soda from my diet, which is a killer to gut health (gut health is foundational to your hormones). I had a hysterosalpingography (HSG), which I believe helped "unblock" my tubes by proxy. There were two iron IV infusion treatments due to low ferritin (but normal iron levels). I outline all the steps that I believe helped me conceive and all that I've learned since then, in my course by the same name -- "Infertility Success." I'm determined to help as many women as I can get to the families of their dreams.

Also not mentioned, the emotional toll month after month of grieving as my period appeared and reappeared. Not to mention months of faking a smile and shrugging off intrusive questions to get through my job. When our oldest son was one, I went on hiatus from my very stressful sales job and, two months later, conceived our twins. It was a financial sacrifice that took us years of adjustments to recover from, but I 100% believe it contributed to their conception.

Only after the fact, and years later, did I realize that I had many, many chemical pregnancies. There were always the tell-tale signs and symptoms of pregnancy, and then I would get my cycle, and they faded away.

> *TIP: Don't discount the little things (coffee, toxins, dehydration, gut health, sleep, stress, exercise); all can dramatically affect the outcome of your procedure and getting pregnant on your own.*

I'll leave you with this. If a doctor tells you **they** can't help you, it doesn't mean you can't get pregnant. I didn't get pregnant because I was special, but because I was willing to exhaust any and all obstacles to build the family of our dreams.

MORE STORIES OF HELP AND HOPE FOR YOUR JOURNEY

Unlock a special video message from Erica and receive a free gift when you scan this code!

Erica Hoke is an Author, Publisher and Infertility Coach on a mission to empower infertility patients and disrupt the reproductive medical system. After being told she had less than a 1% chance of conceiving naturally, Erica refused to give up hope and pursued a different path. She committed to getting to the bottom of her infertility issues via diet, lifestyle changes and traditional Chinese medicine - leading to her becoming a proud mother of four children!

Erica now uses her inspiring story as a means to give hope to those still seeking family through alternate paths. Through free support groups, group coaching opportunities and one-on-one sessions, Erica mentors people through their journeys while teaching them how to collaborate with doctors in order to systematically address their obstacles before pursuing invasive treatments.

For those who have already battled and overcome infertility, Erica offers the chance for healing through book collaborations and sharing stories. Every step forward gives others the strength they need on their own journeys. #NeverGiveUpHope

ACKNOWLEDGMENT

This book would never have been possible without my husband Roy's unwavering support and love. For many years, he held my hand and comforted me through the struggles of infertility. He always believed that we could do it even when I had doubts myself. His generosity, compassion and belief in me gave me the strength to keep going.

To my four beautiful children - Kingston, Bronson, Preston and Holden - you are a miracle of life and an inspiration every single day. I'm so grateful for each one of you and pray that you will come to fully appreciate how extraordinary your lives truly are.

A special thanks goes out to my editor Melissa Denelsbeck for her patience and support and to Meggan Larson for mentoring me through this publishing journey.

Finally, thank you to all the authors who joined us on this project and shared their stories with vulnerability and courage. And most importantly thank you to YOU, dear reader. We are praying for you - we vote for your victory with the breath of God breathed upon you!

#SharingOurStories

www.ingramcontent.com/pod-product-compliance
Lightning Source LLC
Chambersburg PA
CBHW071459080526
44587CB00014B/2150